Turnaround

Turnaround

A Public Sector Story

Shiv Malik

OM

Om Books International

First published in 2010

OM
Om Books International

Corporate & Editorial Office
A-12, Sector 64, Noida 201 301
Uttar Pradesh, India
Phone: +91 120 477 4100

Sales Office
4379/4B, Prakash House, Ansari Road
Darya Ganj, New Delhi 110 002, India
Phone: +91 11 2326 3363, 2326 5303
Fax: +91 11 2327 8091
Email: sales@ombooks.com
Website: www.ombooks.com

Typeset by Mindways Design, New Delhi

ISBN: 978-93-80069-39-5

10 9 8 7 6 5 4 3 2 1

Printed in India

For Pratima
my soulmate and inspiration
who now blossoms in God's own garden

CONTENTS

ACKNOWLEDGEMENTS

I WAS INSPIRED TO WRITE THIS BOOK BY MY LATE WIFE, Dr Pratima Malik.

I am thankful to Sanjiv Batra, the chairman and managing director of MMTC (2010); SD Kapoor, the former CMD; Dr SR Jain, advisor; and other past and present directors, who readily provided me with the latest information about MMTC and Neelachal Ispat Nigam Ltd. (NINL). I am also thankful to Arun Mirchandani, the CMD of PEC and AK Srivastava, the former CMD for their support. The help provided by my old colleagues in the three companies enabled me to be accurate and up-to-date.

I am much grateful to my daughter, Divya Malik Lahiri and son-in-law, Jaideep Lahiri, for painstakingly improving the final draft, making it well-balanced and suggesting the concept of the book; to Kalyani Shankar, J.P. Malik and Mrs Anna R Malhotra, for going through the initial draft and giving their invaluable suggestions; to my friend AS Bhasin, for initiating me into the ways of research and writing books; and to Dr KN Malik, for introducing me to the world of publishing.

I am very grateful to my friend, Meera Sai, with whom I discussed many new ideas contained herein and for her deep conviction that reforms must create new jobs for the youth, reduce poverty and help the affected people.

My 12-year-old grandson, Probir, promptly offered to be the first reader, which inspired me to complete it.

I am also appreciative of the management of the India International Centre and India Habitat Centre for providing me with an intellectual environment to work in.

Preface

THE PUBLIC SECTOR PLAYED A CENTRAL ROLE IN THE development of India till the 1980s and built much of the infrastructure that we now have. It built the commanding heights of the economy. The public sector invested in areas where the private sector feared to tread or did not have the means or the permission, and laid the foundation on which the private sector could build its edifice. It occupied a very prestigious and exalted position in the Indian economy.

But things started changing after the economic reforms were ushered in 1991. The private sector was the favoured hero. As trade and industry were opened to the private sector, the public sector was at the losing end. It lost its monopoly and income streams, but it still had to retain the excessive manpower with its ever-escalating costs. The public sector was clearly on the wrong side of the reforms.

The nineties were stressful, full of turmoil, yet challenging and exciting for the public sector, which pulled its socks to regain respect in the society and find a new place in a competitive globalised world.

While the emphasis shifted to profit and profitability, the government continued to impose social obligations. Thus, instead of a single objective of economic performance, it ended up with a curious jumble of contradictory objectives.

The private sector had the autonomy to deliver the single objective of economic performance, but the government did not grant this autonomy to the public sector enterprises (PSEs). Yet, it expected them to perform.

Unlike the private sector, the PSEs continued to fall under the definition of 'State' and, hence, were accountable to many institutions like the Parliament, Comptroller and Auditor General (CAG) and CBI. Their commercial decisions were also subject to judicial scrutiny.

This made decision making a hostage to a threat of enquiries and investigations, irresponsible public-interest litigation, and widespread fear of ruining the careers of managers in case they took any calculated business risks that failed to pay off. But is there any business which is risk free? When decisions are not made by managers to maximise economic performance but to play safe and guard against investigations, corporate performance is the main victim.

In spite of these handicaps, many PSEs improved performance dramatically after the economic reforms and some of them became the top performers. According to the Public Enterprises Survey of the year 2006–07, the net profit to capital employed ratio improved from 5.44% in 1997–98 to 12.26% in 2006–07. However, while the private sector galloped with the liberalisation of trade and industry and basked in the recognition of its new rising stars, the public sector clearly lost its flavour.

After spending about 26 years in the private sector, I was lucky to be in the ringside seat in the public sector for about a decade during its most challenging and tumultuous period.

Perched in this seat, I had the unique opportunity to be a witness to an interesting interaction among the ministers, politicians, bureaucrats, and public sector officials; between the ministries and the PSEs; amongst the ministries themselves; among individual players within the bureaucracy and the PSEs; and between the PSEs and the media.

It was fascinating to observe how the ego and motives of these players actually played out in their complex interaction with each other and how it affected the performance of these institutions. It was also interesting to watch how personal agendas combined with their official agendas, and how jealousies, rivalries, cronyism, and patronage affected the recruitment to the top jobs engulfing politicians, ministers, bureaucrats, Central Vigilance Commission (CVC), press, and the judiciary. It was, indeed, a very curious milieu.

These assignments gave me an opportunity to watch how the different nations negotiated large-value purchase and sales contracts and how some of them adopted superior purchase processes than those followed in India.

Some innovations in India's buying processes have been suggested herein. I have dealt with negotiations in the global and domestic context, and some practical general guidelines have been suggested that I found useful.

This book also deals with effective decision making, suggests an organisation structure and the practical ways of making quality decisions that can have a positive impact on the destiny of the companies. How the decision on choosing priorities involves courage rather than ability is also brought out in the book. It also highlights the general principles and discipline involved in decision making.

The central theme, however, is the turnaround of the public sector and that of any other organisation or institution. Case studies of MMTC and PEC are focussed upon turnaround within the existing rules and that of NINL and on how to get the rules of the game changed in order to perform. MMTC had lost 80% of its annual business of Rs. 8000 crore (1 crore is equal to 10 million) following the economic reforms of 1991–92 and was left with a rump annual business of Rs. 1500 crore only. However, it transformed itself and recorded an annual turnover of Rs. 45,000 crore in 2009–10. NINL proved a game changer for MMTC and its fascinating story has been narrated herein.

PEC increased its annual business from Rs. 86 crore in 1988–89 to over Rs. 10,000 crore in 2008–09 and won, for six consecutive years, 1998–2004, the Prime Minister's Award for Excellence, for being one of the ten best public sector companies in the Memorandum of Understanding (MOU) performance.

MMTC was also honoured with the Prime Minister's Award for the years 2006–07 and 2007–08 and the National Awards for the highest exports of minerals every year since the early nineties.

The PEC turnaround experience broke me into the ways of the public sector and proved a useful initial preparation for MMTC. The strategies followed were neutral to ownership, whether private or public or whether a company, institution, or an NGO, which could be adapted by any public or private company or an institution depending upon the peculiar ground realities.

The chapters share with you the inside story of how these companies turned around in the face of discontinuity of business and that too within the constraints of the public sector. They bring out the central place of communications, dispersed and well-distributed leadership, team work, and passion for achieving the mission, grit, zeal, and determination in any turnaround situation.

We cannot afford to simply grumble about the problems faced by the public sector or any other organisation. We have to perform and deliver, no matter what. Some practical suggestions on how to work through the system have been indicated here.

The story of NINL, a 1.1 million tons per annum pig iron/steel/metallurgical coke and power plant shows how it was possible to set up new projects despite the state policy being on the contrary. It shows how it is possible to get the policies changed and that of the country; and how everybody comes on the same page if you have a conviction and a missionary spirit to achieve your mission and can communicate it effectively to those who matter.

This is a story of the triumph of the human spirit over adverse environment conditions that can be attempted by any human or institution. It suggests practical ways, within the constraints of the system, to have an interaction between the ministers, bureaucrats, and public sector officials more productive. The private sector managers will also find this story rewarding as they too face many obstacles, which can be surmounted with a similar philosophy.

The chapters on 'Baptism by Fire' and 'The Turnaround of the Public Sector' focus on how to reform and transform the public sector itself, and break fresh ground through suggesting an entrepreneurial solution to the rehabilitation of the surplus staff, instead of just doling out voluntary retirement benefits. A way out has also been suggested for transforming the PSEs.

I have also indicated a road map for the promotion of a new professional sector in the country as it is time to think beyond the traditional public and private sector, since India is going to have the maximum number of young professionals in the world, with the possible exception of China. It indicates the way to carve the professional sector out of the public sector. Independent professionals, scientists, researchers, and academicians could also join this sector. Promotion of such a sector at this juncture can change the face of the country.

This book is neither a treatise on the public sector nor does it try to give a history of the reforms in India. But it does try to identify the major problems and suggests innovative measures. These suggestions will require a national debate as any innovation should.

This book is about leadership and its decentralisation within the organisation and leaving behind leaders who may be bigger and better. Leaders succeed when they start seeing the first signs of leadership in their followers. Followers-turned-leaders alone can ensure the continuity and growth of organisations. My personal beliefs about people and management can be found between the lines in the Turnaround section.

Though MMTC and PEC were PSEs, yet we managed them as commercial enterprises. We could neither have done anything different nor shown more spectacular results had they been private companies. I am sanguine that private sector management could not have provided more freedom to act than the one given by the government in such cases. After all, I worked for more than three decades in the private sector as well.

However, the fact remains that constraints affect a majority of the public sector officers adversely, crippling their performance. Such constraints must be removed through appropriate reforms.

The nation had invested Rs. 4,21,089 crore in the central PSEs as per the Public Enterprises Survey of 2006–07. The investment would be much higher at the current prices. The central PSEs employed about 16.14 lakh people (excluding casual and contract labour) as on March 31, 2006, according to the report. The total public sector employment, including state and departmental government undertakings, self-government institutions and quasi-government bodies, etc. is in the vicinity of 70 lakhs.

Considering the mammoth investment and employment, we need policies and procedures and an enabling environment where the common man, working in this sector, can perform with complete autonomy. Management is all about making ordinary people do extraordinary things.

Though the public sector autonomy and the freedom to decide its own policies, strategies, and investments is not a panacea for turnaround of the public sector, yet this is the minimum condition. But at the end of the day, each company has to find specific solutions to its unique problems and opportunities and this falls under the realm of effective corporate management and good governance irrespective of the ownership issue.

The public sector reforms are absolutely essential if our economy has to fire all cylinders. The question is not whether there should be a private or a public sector. Both the sectors must perform to their optimum capacity.

The public sector companies of India are far better managed than those in the other countries. India must find its own unique solutions and not simply ape the West or blindly follow the recipes of the IMF. Some suggestions have been made in the book.

This book should interest and benefit not only the public sector managers but the private sector managers, professionals, scientists, researchers, academicians, and a large class of budding independent professionals of the country, who would be the biggest beneficiaries of the suggestions contained herein.

1

Baptism by Fire

IN THE LAST JOB I HELD IN THE PRIVATE SECTOR, THE selection and recruitment process involved screening by a selection committee headed by the managing director and the heads of different divisions. Soon after the interview, the candidate was told if he/she was selected. Emoluments were negotiated by the HRD, the same or the next day, and an appointment letter issued soon after. The process took just a day or two. It was perceived to be fair, merit-based, and quick, aimed at selecting leaders who could maximise performance within the ethical values and culture of the company.

Having got used to this, I was surprised at the long and winding selection process in the public sector, which will amuse those peeping into the oddities of life in the Indian public sector.

Here is how it can go:

"I had applied to the Department of Public Enterprises for a suitable senior post in the public sector in the hope that they might call me for an interview for the post of the director of one of the PSEs. I was pleasantly surprised to get an interview call for the post of the chairman and managing director instead. My pleasure and surprise was no less than that of the young man shown in the TV commercial ordering only tea but getting butter, toasts, and biscuits for free.

I was interviewed by the Public Enterprises Selection Board (PESB). Its members were very senior bureaucrats who looked awesome when they asked penetrating questions. It was an interesting situation. I could not fathom the questions by the bureaucrats on business and they could not fathom the answers of a business executive, thanks to our divergent backgrounds. This was a perfect brew. When the wise men discussed merits and demerits of the candidates, they made the mistake of placing me at number one on the panel.

I thought this was it. But I was wrong. I was told that I had not yet made it. The file would be sent to the ACC. I wondered why, as I had not applied for a job to the board of ACC. Then I was told that this ACC was not the company that manufactured cement, but the omnipotent Appointments Committee of the Cabinet headed by the Prime Minister himself. How on earth could the Prime Minister spare time to judge my merit for the post of a chairman of a small PSE? In any case, I felt flattered.

I was assured that they had a foolproof system whereby the Prime Minister and others in the government could judge any person, matter, or issue with the help of a 'briefing'. Whatever was recommended from below in the 'brief' invariably got approved. I wondered why in that case, the government had senior people.

Doubts still lingering in my mind, I ventured to ask how the Prime Minister ensured the selection of the right candidate without meeting him/her. I was reminded that the government had a foolproof system to ensure it. The prime minister's office (PMO) suitably briefed him. I marvelled at the ingenuity of the system.

I then enquired as to when the ACC would meet to discuss my case. They said for such appointments, senior busy bees like the prime minister, the minister of the administrative ministry, the HRD minister, and the home minister, who constituted the ACC, had no time to meet. Therefore, the ACC never met.

Like the tiffin delivered home, the same file was circulated to each member of the ACC for comments or approval. Considering that they took more than three months to decide, I wondered if it would not have been much quicker to circulate me instead.

I also wondered that if these luminaries had no time even to meet and discuss appointments of the public sector, why on earth then were they involved in the selection process.

One day, a wise counsel let me in on a secret. He told me that though the PESB formally selected candidates, the real decision was actually made by the concerned minister on the recommendation made by involved bureaucrats, at the behest of the PMO. This reminded me of the 'Yes Minister' serial on television.

What was then the role of the PESB? If it was merely to make the recommendation for nomination of candidates and that too at the behest of some ministers and bureaucrats, then it would be quicker for them to select and nominate the candidates. Why have the selection board then? I was told someone's recommendation was required to accept or reject a nomination.

My final question proved the last straw on the camel's back. I was told to shut up as I had completely missed the point. I must admit I am still foxed."

The important message to be deduced from this fictional story is that the process of appointment to the top level jobs in the PSEs is seriously flawed and time consuming and results in delays in filling up important positions. Invariably, the process is preceded by a long and dirty succession battle, planting of nasty stories in the media, and raising the issue in the Parliament as well as complaints of corruption to the CVC that can prevent the good candidates from being even considered.

Perpetrators of this offensive usually have close links with the powers that are involved in decision making resulting in meritorious candidates invariably getting sidelined. This is, however, not always true.

Many of the contenders for top jobs are aided and abetted by people who have converted the art of lobbying into an industry. These include businessmen and women, socialites, ministers, god men, and even some retired bureaucrats claiming enough clout.

This process results in a system of cronyism and patronage that debilitates these organisations. It also leads to all kinds of liaisons between the senior executives, politicians, bureaucrats, and vested interests that influence commercial decisions. This is not to say that this happens all the time but whenever it does, it damages the reputation of the organisation and the government.

The quality of the top brass really determines the quality of people in the entire set-up and their values determine the values that would be practised in the company. Therefore, it is important to fix the flawed process of recruitment.

Besides, members of the PESB are senior, able bureaucrats, but most of them do not have hands-on experience of business management.

It would, therefore, be ideal, if instead, retired or serving public sector/private sector chiefs and directors, and professors of management in leading institutes like the IIMs and IITs are appointed members of the selection board. The secretary of the administrative ministry should also be on the board for such appointments. The concerned chairman should be an ex-officio member for the selection of directors of this company. A former or serving senior chairman of a PSE having life-long business experience, should chair this selection board. The chairman and members should be full-time functionaries, who may invite specialists for advice at the time of the interview.

This selection board should be autonomous, its decisions final and binding without any reference to the ACC or the ministry. The appointment letter should be issued within a reasonable time to ensure fair play.

Members should personally check the credentials of the candidates from their previous employers. The past performance should be the criteria for headhunting and it should not merely be a one-time activity. Headhunting should be a continuous process.

The suggested selection process would be thorough, quick, fair, and merit based. The right candidates shall head the public sector undertakings. The present time-consuming process is perceived to be unfair to those who cannot muster political clout, which ultimately leads to debilitating the organisations.

The best way, of course, is to make the public sector companies board-managed, who should directly or through search committees select the right candidates to fill the top jobs. The board best knows the kind of persons required to lead specific functions. This is how it is done in well-managed private companies across the globe.

Once the public sector companies are made board-managed, even the kind of selection board proposed here would not be necessary. And till that happens, such a selection board would serve a useful purpose.

2

Guidelines of Bureau of Public Enterprises and Blinkers

BLINKERS ARE OFTEN WORN AND SHELTER TAKEN UNDER the rigid government rules, procedures, and guidelines issued by the Bureau of Public Enterprises (BPE) for not doing something that is needed.

A file was submitted in MMTC, seeking permission to surrender a commercial plot in the Bandra Kurla complex in Mumbai. The concerned municipal authority had given many notices in the past advising to either start building the complex or surrender the property, but there had been no reaction from MMTC. This had been the final notice.

When it was suggested to start construction within a week, it was stated that a public sector company could not start construction immediately because tenders needed to be floated — a time-consuming procedure. Once the exercise of floating tenders was over, the contract could be given only to the one that quoted the lowest rates. Besides, even this could not be achieved without the basic homework, like preparing plans and specifications. Failure to abide by the procedure could lead to serious implications for the concerned officers.

But since one was determined not to surrender the valuable plot, a meeting had been requisitioned to overcome the anomaly. It was thus decided to:

- Separate the minor work of piling from the major work of construction, as the former could start fast and involved little investment;
- Float short-term tenders confined to public sector construction companies. Place an order with a PSE within the next 4/5 days so that there would be no allegations of making money from private companies. The successful bidder should start digging the next day to meet the one-week deadline imposed by the municipal authority;
- Preparatory work like preparing specifications of the building and tender conditions, etc. should start soon after. This tender involving a major part of the total investment was open to all companies.

This was done. The digging started within a week. This saved the plot and, soon after, an eight-story building was constructed in the now prestigious Bandra Kurla complex. This asset commands today a premium of about Rs. 1000 crore.

The blinker in this case was the false assumption that because of the time-consuming tender procedure, it was difficult for a public sector company to start construction on this plot within a week. Once we took off our blinkers, we divided the tender into two parts that enabled us to start the construction within a week and that too within the tender procedure.

Often the main obstacle lies in our own minds.

THE GUIDELINES OF THE BUREAU OF PUBLIC ENTERPRISES

Right Decision or Right Procedure

The public sector officers grumble about the constraints imposed by the procedures and rules. First, there is a room for flexibility by just thinking about a procedure in a new way as done in the previous case; second, if a wrong procedure comes in the way of doing a right thing, it is our responsibility to get the procedure amended or changed; and third, if it takes excessive time to get the procedure changed, just do the right thing and record your reasons for departing from the procedure.

The important thing is to take the right decision even if the procedure has to be sacrificed. Do what is best in the interest of the company and the country and what adds value. Procedures are made by men/women and can be and must be changed by them. But never ever sacrifice a right decision at the altar of a right procedure, no matter what.

Do not be constrained by the guidelines

Much ado is made about the guidelines of the BPE and how it constrains the performance of the public sector.

All one needs to ensure is that the decisions add value to the company, the employees, and the country and the highest standards of integrity and effectiveness be followed. All obstacles have to be removed. Normally in such cases, neither the Department of Public Enterprises nor the ministry comes in the way or objects to non-adherence to procedures. There was only one exception to this.

PEC was given the responsibility of developing the exports of Indian defence equipment. It recruited a major general who had just retired, as an advisor, to help organise the defence exports at a royal salary of Rs. 4000 per month. PEC received a letter from one of the officers in the ministry saying that according to the rules, it should have paid the general Rs. 2000 per month only, since he was getting his pension too. It was directed to dispense with his services.

The general's skills were appropriate and useful in defence exports and none of the existing officers of the company possessed this competency. PEC did not want to lose the services of a man of his calibre. Therefore, it decided to ignore the letter. However, it had to relent after it was ordered by the ministry to request the general to resign.

The public sector lost his services for a paltry sum. He got a better job with a private company. The management cut a sorry figure with the general and the new assignment of defence exports suffered.

But one should not blame the government for it. Somebody in the ministry made an ego issue out of it and saw it through. It was certainly embarrassing to let the general go. But in this story, the main fault was that of the management. It should have persuaded the minister to apply the necessary corrective.

There is a need to recognise that the guidelines of the BPE are merely guidelines and they are not the office orders, which have a greater force. With good reason, it is possible to depart from these. Even office orders are not sacrosanct; they can be changed if they become outdated. Most orders and guidelines in the government, the public and private sectors are products of their context and time; they outlive their context but nobody reviews them to amend or delete them.

These guidelines need to be changed with the passage of time for which someone has to bell the cat, confident that the deviation is bona fide, in the interest of the company, its people, the society, and is going to add value. One has to go ahead full throttle till somebody pulls the brakes. One seldom gets challenged because of an in-built inertia in human nature. The government seldom questions such well-meaning decisions, and it is possible to get post-facto approval, if required.

However, if somebody is hell-bent to harm, nothing can stop the process. Therefore, why not do what one thinks is right for the company?

How outdated these guidelines have become is borne out by the N Vittal Committee Report, which recommended outright deletion of 762 out of the existing 892 guidelines and dismissed the government's control on functioning of the PSEs and recommended a code of ethics both for the PSEs and the government. But this proved a damp squib as the government did not have the mindset to reduce control, and it continues to be so.

However, the government is unlikely to challenge a decision if taken in the interest of the company.

Here is an example:

MMTC had a trading office in Singapore which needed to be converted into a full-fledged company to make it autonomous and free from the usual constraints.

A wholly owned subsidiary of MMTC, MMTC Transnational Pte Ltd. (MTPL), was established in Singapore in 1994 with a very small staff consisting of a managing director; a deputy general manager, finance; a general sales manager; all temporarily promoted on deputation from amongst the existing officers, and one local assistant. Basically, the existing branch office was converted into a full-fledged company.

The question arose whether the PESB should be informed about the selection of a managing director for this subsidiary and it was unanimously decided that this was not necessary. It just amounted to a mere transfer from one office to the other. The board was taken into confidence and the ministry was kept in the loop.

During 2008–09, this subsidiary having 13 employees, had an annual turnover of US$687 million, paid back more than the equity of US$1 million in the form of dividends to the parent company, a profit after tax of US$6.8 million and a very respectable net worth of US$15 million. Now, it is one of the leading foreign trading companies of Singapore. It no longer is a mere cost centre but a profit centre.

The experiment proved an excellent ground for training senior managers for assuming higher responsibility in the parent company. One of its managing directors, Sanjiv Batra, served as the chairman and managing director of MMTC and another one, Adarsh Goyal, was a board member till recently.

The first general sales manager of MTPL, NK Mathur, who had done the main spadework under the brilliant leadership of YN Bhargava, the then managing director, is now the chairman and managing director of State Trading Corporation (STC) that had a business of Rs. 18,700 crore during 2008–09. Mathur was also the general manager, commercial, of NINL, pig iron/steel company promoted by MMTC, in their formative years. STC is the mother company whose projects and equipment division was converted later into PEC and minerals and metals division into MMTC. These success stories have been chronicled in this book.

The main point, however, is that the decision to deviate from the standard guidelines and procedures that the PESB should select the managing director of a public sector company was respected by the government. Why? Because the move added value to the company and was in the right direction, closer to the vision of becoming a global company. It was done in a transparent manner. Only meritorious persons were posted there, the board was taken into confidence, and the ministry informed.

Another example:

Paying higher emoluments than permissible to the managing director of Neelachal Ispat Nigam Ltd.

MMTC was to set up a pig iron and steel plant in a joint venture. This was a trading company with no experience of manufacturing steel. A new managing director was needed for this project. Dr SR Jain, former chairman of Steel Authority of India Limited (SAIL), who was its advisor, recommended Dr Subroto Ray, a former managing director of the Bhilai Steel Plant, who was working as an executive director in a private company since his retirement from SAIL. An invitation was extended to him to visit Delhi and meet the executive committee of the board. The committee met him for half an hour and everybody was impressed with his experience.

Though he was getting higher emoluments in the private sector, Subroto had requested for a salary lesser than what he was getting but more than the public sector grades plus perks attached to a director. He wanted to join as he felt more comfortable in the public sector environment and was keen to move to Orissa, his home state, where we were setting up this project. He was anxious to look after his ailing mother who was living in Bhubaneswar (Orissa).

The question arose as to how we could pay much higher emoluments to him than enjoyed by the chairman and directors of the parent company. The fact that he knew his job which none of the other incumbents did and therefore deserved better emoluments was brought to the notice of the executive committee.

The committee decided that the public sector salaries were not applicable to this post since the organisation was going to manufacture steel in a joint venture company with the other partners that might include private companies too. It unanimously agreed to recruit Subroto on his terms. And the decision was conveyed to Subroto with a request to take charge within the next two weeks.

The next day, the minister was briefed about this recruitment and the emoluments decided. He did not raise any objection. The government never objected to it because it was felt that the decision was bona fide and necessary, in the interest of the company and the country.

Efforts Made in the Past to Dilute or Delete Some Guidelines of the Bureau of Public Enterprises

Some efforts have been made in the past, as mentioned previously, to review the guidelines of the BPE. The most serious effort was made by the N Vittal Committee in September, 1997, which recommended outright deletion of 762 out of the existing 892 guidelines and recommended a sunset clause and a code of ethics for the public sector and the government. This shows how guidelines become outdated with the change in context over time.

The United Front (UF) Government agreed to cancel 696, modify 25, but still retained 171 guidelines. However, with the streamlined guidelines issued by the government, it has still retained its control in crucial areas like powers of the board of directors, appointment of chairmen and directors, both full time and part time, formulation of voluntary retirement schemes, and creation of posts, decisions on fresh employment, deputation, and house rent, etc.

Amongst the guidelines retained are the prerogative of the government to consider and take decisions on Annual Confidential Reports (ACRs) in case of disputes between officers and the CMD. What is worse is that the retained guidelines contain crucial powers through which the government continues to direct the PSEs on the most important aspects of corporate management, according to MM Luther in his excellent book *Public Sector Reforms — Myths and Realities*. This compromises the autonomy of the public sector.

Luther had been my able predecessor. He was the first chairman of PEC Ltd. He played a crucial role in the formation and building of this company during its infancy.

The public sector should be proactive in getting the remaining guidelines that impinge on its autonomy abolished or amended, so that it is not prevented from taking right decisions expeditiously.

In any case, a right decision should not be sacrificed for the sake of a right procedure. Such decisions should preferably be taken in the board committees and the board should consult the ministry; or simply record the reasons for deviating from a guideline and assume the responsibility for such decisions, if there is courage of conviction. One precaution needed is to make sure that there is no adverse boss who has demonstrated his/her ability to go out of the way to cause damage. But in such an eventuality, this kind of a boss shall find another rope to hang them, whether they deviate from a guideline or not.

3

TURNAROUND OF PEC LTD.

I WORKED AS THE CHAIRMAN AND MANAGING DIRECTOR, Projects & Equipment Corporation of India Ltd., which later became PEC Ltd., from January 1989 to May 1992 before joining MMTC for five years in the same capacity. However, the association with PEC continued for another year as an additional charge even after joining MMTC. Both these companies were undertakings of the Ministry of Commerce.

PEC had suffered a huge set back. The then Prime Minister, Rajiv Gandhi, was unhappy with the performance, as during his visit, the Indonesian President had complained about unsatisfactory results in establishing the cement plant at Padang, and demanded a compensation of about Rs. 11 crore that had to be remitted by PEC on the PM's return to India. PEC was a small company and could ill-afford such a heavy penalty.

One of the contractors engaged by PEC abandoned it mid-course and the organisation was left with no choice but to complete the project as a leader of the consortium that had provided a performance guarantee. The responsibility of each player of the consortium was joint and individual, and the errant contractor was punished by the government of India by denying to it the export benefits. Yet, as the leader of the consortium, PEC had to pay the penalty.

However, the PEC officers had actually contracted the project so well that even after paying the penalty, the company made a reasonable profit.

Had the government not intervened, this would probably have been just another commercial dispute as the Indonesian cement project authorities had not fulfilled some of their obligations as well, making it difficult for the Indian party to execute the job on time.

The previous chairman was given the marching orders and a few other officers were put in the dock, though they worked hard to salvage this project. Sometimes, one just runs out of luck. PEC lost the confidence of the prime minister and everyone else in the bureaucracy. The briefing given to me at the time of joining mirrored the same opinion.

PEC was set up by the government of India in April, 1971, for setting up projects abroad and helping the engineering industry of India to export engineering equipment by carving out the projects and equipment division of the State Trading Corporation (STC). Its annual turnover, which was Rs. 116 crore in 1986, had been gradually falling and had shrunk to Rs. 85 crore in 1989. The rate of return on investment was only 3.5%. The Indonesian crisis, which the company faced at the top of these problems, raised questions about its viability.

It was a subsidiary of STC at that time, though it was reporting directly to the commerce minister. However, during my tenure, the government decided to make it an autonomous company and it ceased to be a subsidiary. The government experimented with establishing a holding company, Bharat Business International Ltd., for STC, MMTC, and PEC. SVS Raghavan, a former chairman of MMTC, was appointed its chairman. However, this experiment lasted for a few months only and it was wound up.

The belief that PEC should be a subsidiary of a bigger company was rooted in the false assumption that it was not financially strong enough to stand on its own. The government recognised that it was a false assumption and set it right.

CHALLENGING BUSINESS ASSUMPTIONS PLACED IT ON A HIGHER TRAJECTORY

PEC had introduced many Indian engineering exporters to various foreign markets, but the moment they were in direct touch, most of them bypassed it and approached the customers directly, to save the frugal service charges (commission). This ate into the repeat sale. Therefore, the annual business gradually went down.

There were murmurs that PEC would be wound up. But the government decided to make fresh appointments at the top.

The People

Gross introspection followed. There was nothing wrong with the people, and some of them could be counted amongst the best in the land. An earlier CMD, MM Luther, responsible for converting the projects and equipment division of STC into a separate company, had done a great job by ensuring that only engineers and their private secretaries and some assistants move to PEC. His successors neither increased the number of employees nor the character of the company. Consequently, there were about 250 odd employees including many engineers, which was a pleasant surprise for a public sector environment. Nothing really was the matter with the human resources, so the search began to find out the root cause of the dwindling fortunes.

SIMPLE STEPS TO IMPROVE SALES, PROFIT, AND PROFITABILITY

Business Analysis

We looked at the profitability but did not like it one bit. The manufacturers who exported through PEC looked at its service charges as an unnecessary cut on their profit.

One day, we examined the exhaustive list of services provided to the associate suppliers/manufacturers. It was decided to price these services and demand only a legitimate profit. When this was done, the officers developed new confidence in the value of their services and became bolder in demanding a higher service charge from the associates. This helped increase profit.

The board empowered junior officers to finalise contracts if they could do it at higher service charges without taking approval from the senior officers, which acted as a great morale booster for the relatively junior managers. Even the senior officers were more careful now in demanding higher service charges to retain leadership within their departments. This helped increase the profit.

Agents were appointed to pursue tenders invited by foreign government authorities. It was found that sometimes the profit of agents exceeded the share of the company. To reduce this weakness in negotiations, it was decided that the share of the company had to be higher than that of the agents.

Such simple measures helped change the mindset of officers in favour of a higher profitability.

Concentration of Resources

It was a small company and had a limited budget for travelling at that time but to officers were travelling in many countries in Asia, the Middle East, Europe, USA, Africa, South America, and the then USSR. This was spreading the butter too thin.

To improve concentration of resources, it was decided to make only five countries as thrust areas, which would ensure maximum returns on travel expenses, rather than spreading the net to encompass all the countries. This strategy increased sales dramatically resulting in improved profits. For example, in countries like Bangladesh and Mauritius, exports increased from about Rs. 2 to 3 crore per annum to over Rs. 40 crore in just one year.

Concentration and focus on a few priorities is one of the best strategies that seldom fails to give great results unless the focus itself is wrong.

Rectifying the Business Processes

The repaired processes included finding customers, generating enquiries, preparing commercial offers in time, negotiating contracts with the supporting manufacturer associates and engineering and project contractors before submitting our bids, pursuing our offers through increased contact with the customers, securing orders, getting the orders executed and delivered in time by a detailed follow up with the associates, and securing completion certificates and payment from the customers in time.

Simple Management Information System

A simple management information system (MIS) was devised to monitor and improve the bidding rate against the foreign tenders, which ensured a brisk follow up of the proposals submitted and the accountability of the officers.

It was discovered that many a times, the concerned sales division got too little time to quote and hence could not offer the bid. There was one expensive international magazine that published good global tenders and enquiries. The single copy would then be circulated from one department to the other, resulting in a delay. So the process of photocopying the magazine was initiated, and distributed simultaneously to all the sales divisions. This simple step improved the rate of bidding considerably, and helped to boost sales.

Monitoring Performance

The performance of the company was constantly monitored on commonly agreed objectives through frequent communication meetings. This helped people to keep their eye on the ball all the time.

Putting the Finger at the Critical Parameter for Increasing Sales

It was discovered that our shipments/sales were more dependent on the backlog of orders carried over from the previous year than the orders booked in the current year, because the manufacture of equipment and its shipment required time and project execution was spread over a longer time horizon. Therefore, increased concentration on amassing as much of carried forward orders as possible became necessary. This was the critical factor determining sales/shipments. This also helped improve forecasting of the top line. It was not safe to include in our forecast for the top line all the orders booked during the current year, because we could not be sure of its manufacture and supply.

These steps helped improve sales, profits, and profitability. Yet, there was a need to scale up faster.

Scaling Up

Flirting with cotton led PEC into trading of commodities

It was learnt from a visiting Vietnamese delegation of textile mills that it had floated a tender for cotton that would close within a day. Since PEC was not dealing with non-engineering goods like cotton, a contact was established with the chairman of Cotton Corporation of India. While it agreed to make provision for a 5% service margin for PEC, it was not ready to risk shipping it to the desired port of Vietnam. PEC agreed to assume the risk of shipping for an additional service charge of 2.5%.

Quotations were submitted for the first time against a tender for cotton. PEC Hanoi, Vietnam, called the same day to inform about the successful bid, and emphasised the need for confirmation, and submission of a performance bond for delivering the entire quantity of cotton costing about Rs. 17 crore within two months, failing which, there was a penalty clause for each day of delay.

PEC knew nothing about cotton but a deal was signed.

A pilot for cotton

A task force of about six officers was formed by pulling out engineers from the mechanical, electrical, and territory divisions and assigned the responsibility of overseeing supply from 24 collection centres in the cotton producing regions of India within 45 days. A contract was signed with an international inspection agency which deputed 10–12 inspectors to test the quality to customer's specifications. The brief was to ensure that the supply was received by the customer in good condition, within the stipulated time of two months.

The team completed the task well on time and the payments were duly received from the customer. This experience sufficed to indicate PEC's trading ability, irrespective of the nature of the product.

A killing of sorts had been made in this deal. But more importantly, it opened a new window for trading in commodities like rice, wheat, soya meal, sugar, gold and industrial raw materials like coal, minerals, and metals that later catapulted PEC into a much higher trajectory. A major constraint on business was thus removed. This experience became the footboard for experimenting with new ideas.

Challenging the Assumptions of PEC

Now the basic assumptions of the company and the government charter constraining growth became the parameters for serious deliberations. Thus far, the charter was to export engineering goods, equipment, and projects only. The underlying assumptions were the following:

1. PEC would export only.

In other words, it will not import or sell in the domestic market, which is a severe constraint on the income and growth of a trading company. This assumption was challenged and experiment to import and sell in the domestic market was undertaken, which broadened the income base.

The mainstay of PEC today is not exports, but imports. This was the infraction, a point when the attention was diverted to imports and domestic sales. In the year 2007–08, the import turnover of the company was about Rs. 4347 crore and the domestic trading was about Rs. 421 crore as compared to practically zilch before 1989–90. The exports during the same year were about Rs. 903 crore, much less than its imports.

2. The products permitted by the government to export were only engineering equipment and projects.

In other words, it could not export or import commodities like cotton, sugar, fertilisers, wheat, rice, industrial raw materials, minerals and metals, bullion, and many other products.

These products fell under the charter of the big sister companies, MMTC and STC, which were undertakings of the same ministry. But the big sister companies were dealing with engineering products too. PEC questioned their selling of engineering products and projects. Many meetings took place amongst the officers of the government, PEC, STC, and MMTC about restricting each of the three sister companies to their respective charters, but they failed. In view of this, PEC went ahead with its experiments to deal with non-engineering products.

Challenging this assumption changed the dimensions of PEC. The initial successes were in the export of cotton and import of scrap and coal on behalf of the customers. But later, it engulfed the entire product range making PEC a general trading company and catapulting its annual turnover to Rs. 5671 crore in 2007–08. During the year 2008–09, PEC expected to achieve a turnover of over Rs. 7000 crore, according to the annual reports and releases of the company. The name of the company was also changed from Projects & Equipment Corporation of India Ltd. to PEC Ltd. to reflect the new character of the company.

This was a long jump from the days when its annual turnover had fallen to Rs. 85 crore in 1988–89.

3. The third assumption was that PEC was a projects organisation like an EPC contractor.

It was discovered that PEC had not executed projects in India but had completed many projects abroad. This was an anomaly because PEC was actually good at trading in projects, bidding, contracting, and securing the order. However, when it came to execution, dependence was only on associate contractors, who would construct and establish these projects. PEC managers were good at coordinating and supervising them and assuming the responsibility of getting the projects completed in time and then getting the completion certificate and payment from the customers. This qualified PEC to be termed as a project trading company, but not an engineering and project constructor (EPC).

PEC also challenged the assumption that it was a projects organisation and the government was appraised in no uncertain terms that it did not have the project execution skills. Therefore, there should be no expectations of skills of a projects organisation or an EPC contractor. This was evident in the Indonesian cement project.

The government was measuring the performance of PEC on the false assumption that it was a project construction company. Hence there was a mismatch between the expectations and the actual performance, raising questions on the very survival and purpose of the company.

PEC stopped trying to become or project itself as an engineering projects construction company and this helped tone down the expectations, thus allowing it to concentrate on the main competency of exporting engineering goods, and experimenting with the imports and domestic selling of commodities and other goods. It decided to become a general international trading company. This was a major shift for growth in the right direction and in redefining what it was.

4. The fourth assumption of PEC was that it could survive only as a subsidiary of its principal company.

This assumption was because it was wrongly thought that PEC did not have the sufficient financial muscle to stand on its own. The government recognised that PEC was a financially self-reliant organisation and hence made it a totally independent company. This encouraged PEC to put up a stellar performance as it was keen to prove that it could not only survive as an independent company, but prosper too.

An important lesson that every business/company must learn is to re-examine its basic assumptions and constraints from time to time. Often the assumptions of business become invalid over time when the context changes. Substituting the invalid assumptions with the valid ones removes major constraints on its business and is one of the most powerful ways to dramatically increase business.

Similarly, it pays to examine the constraints which restrict business. Their removal too can dramatically improve the performance. In PEC, the false assumptions themselves were the major constraints on its business and were about to stifle it.

Sometimes, the constraints for the firms originate from the industry in which they are operating, which requires coordinated thinking and action by the industry.

In about a year, PEC had reversed the four-year trend of falling sales. In another year-and-a-half, the top line more than doubled, order booking tripled, and our rate of return on investment increased from about 3.5% to 13.5%.

In the next 13 years down the line, under individuals like AK Srivastava, who presided over the company's affairs for nine years and Arun Mirchandani, the top line exceeded Rs. 10,000 crore, profit after tax Rs. 65 crore and reserves and surplus Rs. 175 crore during the year 2008–09. It also paid a dividend at the rate of 450% of the paid up capital in 2007–08, which was on top of dividend of 350% in 2006–07 and 150% in 2005–06. PEC had the unique honour of receiving the Prime Minister's Award for best MOU performance continuously for five years since 1998–99.

The engineering and projects business of the company in all these years has not increased much and forms a small percentage of the total trading. Had it not questioned the assumptions of the company and the original mandate of the government, the company might have been extinct by now or at least on life support. This would have happened, notwithstanding the fact that PEC won the National Exports Award for the highest exports of engineering equipment year after year.

WHAT LED TO THE METAMORPHOSIS OF PEC

Competent Team

First and foremost, PEC had a very capable team of dedicated and self-driven engineers, officers and their supporting staff. Their self-respect had been badly hurt as they felt that they had been criticised undeservedly for the Indonesian Cement Project. They were anxious to redeem their honour.

Support of the Entrepreneurial Spirit

We appreciated their skills, devotion, ability and hard work and projected it honestly to the government. Under the circumstances, they needed somebody to hold their hands, support them and apply a balm on their hurt pride. A proactive and entrepreneurial team was needed, which enjoyed experimentation. Such a team would necessarily make mistakes. Nobody in the public sector can afford to experiment if he/she is going to be thrown to the wolves even in the case of a genuine mistake. Therefore, their entrepreneurial efforts were supported to the hilt.

Communication — the Heart and Soul of Transformation

PEC through scheduled communication meetings of officers from all the departments evolved a new MIS, which measured and assessed the performance of each divisional team.

Such communication meetings provide the forum for thrashing out the vision and mission of the company; identifying the ground realities; defining the present and future business; determining the strategy for moving from where you are to where you want to go and allocating the necessary resources; brain storming on new suggestions and ideas, assessing the group and individual performance; transferring the successful initiatives and practices of one sales division to the other; and forming inter-divisional task forces to handle new products, strategic initiatives that inculcate team spirit, a sense of joint responsibility and ownership.

These meetings were also a forum for fights and their resolution between the sales, finance, HR, administration, and the sales divisions, and where officers brought up whatever assistance they needed to achieve their goals.

The meetings were a source of great education for all the officers. They personally heard from the senior people what the priorities were, how performance was assessed, and above all, how senior people made decisions. This was the nursery for developing leaders through the length and breadth of the company.

Above all, these interactive sessions helped develop a common idea of the company, an understanding of its core competence, a common mission, and an agreement on the objectives, strategy, and action plans. They brought down the departmental walls and promoted an open and frank dialogue between the senior and junior officers.

Business Orientation of the Company

Scheduled communication sessions helped bring about business orientation. Weekly progress of each division and the various officers assigned to different assignments needed to be monitored against targets very closely. As a result, everybody in the company would have his/her eye on the ball.

Process Improvements

Work processes like presales, sales, making arrangements and agreements with the supporting associates, execution, shipments, delivery and collection of debtors, etc. were repaired to bring about optimum results.

Inter-Divisional Task Forces and Teams

PEC was not a very bureaucratic organisation, partly because the number of employees was comparatively small and practically everyone was in touch with the senior management. But the differences in perception were reflected in the files delaying decision making. While the sales division would adopt a more aggressive posture, the finance division could negate it ostensibly to moderate the aggressiveness of the former.

In order to solve this problem, the practice of making joint teams consisting of the sales and the finance divisions was started. These joint teams would visit the customers in various countries, whenever it was suspected that the two departments would not agree. The team was made jointly responsible for the result. This enabled the finance officials to get an exposure to the problems raised by the customers and solve them on the spot.

Fortunately, the head of the finance department, late SL Gupta, had a great understanding of the marketing angle. He ensured that his team embraced the company's perspective instead of the finance perspective. Before long, the departmental outlook gave way to the customer/company perspective.

Concentration of Resources on a Few Countries

Since there was a small budget for travelling, focussing it on just five countries helped increase the sales manifold. Later on, it started operating in many countries when PEC had more resources.

Communication with the Government/Shareholders

The process of constant communication and dialogue had been opened with the government directors on the board and other senior officers of the ministry. In fact, interaction with them on new initiatives resulted in making them part of PEC's dreams. Consequently, the government started realising the worth of PEC officers and the contribution they were making. Keeping the ministry officials/shareholders informed of the small and big successes helped them appreciate the positive changes taking place in the company.

Gone was the prejudice against PEC. The government started projecting it as an example of turnaround.

A willing cooperation from the officers, staff, and the unions of PEC, and the officials and ministers of the commerce ministry went a long way in bringing about the changes.

Entrepreneurship and Customer Orientation

The company encouraged entrepreneurship, experimentation, aggressive selling, and an increased personal contact with the customers through visits. This helped increase sales. Inside the company, the process of cost analysis and incorporating all the costs including that of the risk in our proposals to the customers was encouraged, in addition to a higher profit margin. This improved profit and profitability.

The addition of defence exports to the business portfolio helped increase the sales further. Excellent support was received from the secretaries of the Departments of Defence and Defence Production.

Challenging the Assumptions of the Company and Removing Constraints

But the one factor that changed the dimension was challenging the assumptions of the company and removing the constraints they imposed. This brought in structural changes, made PEC a general international trading company, and multiplied its income many fold.

Working within the norms of the existing public sector policies and rules did not cause any problem in transforming PEC. The ownership of the company, public or private, made no difference to its performance.

At the end of the day, each PSE has to behave like any other commercial enterprise, and it is the effective management, good corporate governance, development of leadership throughout the company, and competent execution that makes the ultimate difference. This is all we did to bring about the turnaround of PEC.

The experience of PEC proved an essential preparation for me to deal with MMTC.

4

TRANSFORMATION OF MMTC

MINERALS AND METALS TRADING CORPORATION OF INDIA, which later became MMTC Ltd., was carved out of STC by spinning out its minerals and metals division in 1963. I joined the organisation in May 1992 as the chairman and managing director for a term of five years and simultaneously held the same position in PEC for another year.

THE OTHER SIDE OF THE TRADE REFORMS

The economic reforms of July 1991 were like a bull charging into a china shop with all its fury. MMTC was left gasping for breath as it lost 80% of its business in quick succession. I was given the mandate to collect the debris and rejoin it in the best possible manner to sustain the 5000 odd employees, even as its income got transferred to private traders following opening of the trade. With little or no option left, one tried to divert the attention to whatever was spared, which was frustrating because it meant destroying at least one-fourth of the remaining 20% rump business. Besides that, there were other problems.

The uncollected sundry debtors of over Rs. 1700 crore were crying hoarse not only for collection but for a complete overhaul of the work processes and quality of business transaction. The internal bureaucracy had to make way for entrepreneurship and experimentation that would require new ways of working, thinking, and changed habits and attitudes. All this would need a new system of support for the employees.

Added to this was the problem of inventory of over Rs. 700 crore, which called for a complete overhaul of buying, selling, and money management processes. As one can say, troubles seldom come alone.

Fundamental Questions

There was a need to look at the elementary questions raised by Peter F. Drucker, said to be the father of modern management: What was the business, what is the business, and what should be the business, and how to migrate from what is to what should be?

The other haunting question was how to save the jobs and ensure financial security in the face of vanishing income and cash flow, but ever-escalating expenses. The doomsday Cassandras had already written the epitaph. Consequently, the morale of the employees was abysmally low.

Dialogue for Survival

An in-house debate to find answers to these troubling questions was initiated. To start with, the silence of the people was deafening. But the reticence gradually broke as the need to engage in an honest dialogue (where everyone had a voice) was realised. More and more people started communicating. This to and fro dialogue helped the management find answers.

To begin with, it was understood that MMTC's main business was international trade in all products. So new products, that had a major presence in the export and import basket, were developed. The name of the company was changed from Minerals and Metals Trading Corporation of India Ltd. to MMTC Ltd., as a step in the right direction.

However, there was not much headway being made in marketing fashion garments and leather goods, as the set-up lacked the temperament to do such trading. It was realised that the business was not international trade in *any* product but in *bulk products* like fertilisers, minerals, non-ferrous metals, gold and silver, and agro products. MMTC had the aptitude for bulk handling and its associated activities like warehousing, movement, transport and shipping, etc. Once this realisation dawned on the management, it decided to stick to trading in bulk handling of products alone. However, the crude oil-based products had to be abandoned because there was a lack in the infrastructure for handling them.

The communication sessions became a major source of transformation of the company. These meetings achieved a sharp definition of the mission, vision, core competency, and concept. Further they demolished departmental walls and bureaucracy. They also helped in training young leaders in decision making, monitoring and performance assessment, building peer pressure, achieving consensus and conflict resolution.

Structure for Communication and Decision Making

The structured communication meetings in MMTC included a Directors' Committee consisting of all full-time directors and the chairman. Any issue could be raised by any director with or without an agenda. The discussion was informal. This committee was approved by the board, and brought about informality at the board level. Sensitive issues got discussed in an informal manner.

The second forum was an already existing Sales and Purchase Committee that decided on all major purchase and sales matters and millions of dollars worth of materials were ordered based on its decisions. It met once or twice a week.

The third group formed was called the Investment Committee. It evaluated investment decisions before they were sent to the government for approval. It decided on joint ventures, wholly owned subsidiaries, other investments in India and abroad, including development of trade-related infrastructure. Only the chairman and full-time internal directors constituted this committee and the board had delegated to it the authority to approve an investment in equity of up to $2 million in a joint venture or otherwise. This decision proved a big boost to the development of entrepreneurship.

A fourth committee was constituted for the purpose of performance evaluation and promotions which met once or twice a year. Every full-time director became a member of this committee, though earlier only a few directors were its members. This was done to emphasise consensus within the organisation, get a wider perspective, and deeper knowledge of the candidates to be promoted.

The fifth communication hub was the fortnightly communication meeting in the head office where the chairman, full-time directors, senior- and middle-level officers from all the sales divisions, finance, corporate planning and public relations, etc. were represented. This was a structured meeting on the fortnightly performance of the company. It dwelt on the strategies being followed, state of competition, difficulties being faced, assumptions of the market, and what performance could be realistically expected from various sales divisions and officers. This meeting also brought out the help required by each division from other colleagues and top management.

Parallel fortnightly communication meetings were held in the branches by the general managers.

It was mainly the fortnightly communication meetings which brought about informality and frankness and broke down all departmental walls and from where the management drew its cues for further action. The top management modified its strategy after getting a reality check from this meeting. This ensured practical decisions rooted in ground realities of the company and the market and resulted in tremendous peer pressure on the organisation. Nobody could pass on the buck to anybody else since all responsible officers were present there to defend their own turf.

Good experiments by one group quickly spread to the rest of the organisation through such communication meetings.

The board committees, fortnightly communication meetings, and other unstructured communication meetings were not only the mechanism for the free flow of communication but were together the mechanism for decision making. The board of directors was, of course, the top decision-making body.

Once this decision-making structure was in place, momentous decisions were quick even in a public sector environment. Most decisions could not normally be questioned.

Every company can decide its own peculiar structure for decision making and communications depending on its specific circumstances, but it is important to have one for effectiveness.

The Chief Executive Team Concept

MMTC practised the concept of a 'chief executive team' instead of a 'chief executive officer' as management of large companies had become a complex job, which needed a chief executive team and not merely one CEO. The board of directors is supposed to be the chief executive team, but in actual practice, if it is not involved in all major decisions or not empowered to act in this manner, it fails to be effective.

The practice of this concept did help in reconciling differences at the top level which sent the right cues to the rest of the organisation. Besides, each director acted not only as a CEO of a division, but participated in making decisions for the entire company in various committees, which were otherwise made by the chairman and managing director or the individual director of the concerned division. This also gave an opportunity to the directors to express an opinion on the work relating to each other's divisions and promoted a company perspective instead of a departmental one. It also prepared the directors to assume higher responsibilities.

Work Allocation

Each director was allotted the responsibilities and product areas in which he was relatively more competent and the CMD kept with him vital areas which he thought he could handle better than the others.

By and large, while the current operations were allotted to the directors, the CMD decided to perform the following functions: making the future and driving growth, setting the tone, values and direction of the company, helping in finalising targets in relevant result areas and strict monitoring of the current operations and targets, setting the score and acting as independent score keeper and a neutral referee, managing borderline relations, and maintaining a balance between the present and the future of the company.

BUILDING BLOCKS OF TRANSFORMATION

Staying with Old Skills

Despite the loss of monopoly, the management decided to stay with the old products, import them with its own resources, and then sell them through their own sales force and a network of dealers and distributors. The inherent advantage of this philosophy was that the organisation did not lose the product skills of its employees and maintained continuity, though the challenge of teaching market skills, developing a distribution network, and risk mitigation skills still persisted.

Joint Ventures for New Products and Trade-Related Infrastructure

The next building block for securing a hold on the products was to invest in joint ventures and take in return share of the products manufactured. It was also decided to build trade-related infrastructure in joint ventures. Initial experiments/pilots made with minority shareholding in two or three small joint ventures, with management control in the hands of the private sector partners, did not yield any results. So, the realisation dawned that it was important to have management control of the joint ventures. This brought about positive results when it came to major joint venture investment in the pig iron/steel/met coke/power complex, involving a total project cost of about Rs. 2000 crore. This project was not only an instant success but changed the fate of MMTC.

Making Company Customer/Market Centric

In the slogan *'Move from government-led growth to market-led growth'*, the employees got the right message that growth would not come in the future through grant of monopoly by the government but from the market and, therefore, they have to satisfy the customers.

The employees were motivated to make the company customer-centric, market-centric, and competitor-centric. All the directors including director of finance and director HRD were allocated certain territories where they were supposed to meet important customers to acquaint themselves with their problems and opportunities. Even director vigilance was asked to visit certain customers so that he could appreciate the reality of the customers before giving judgements on vigilance cases. The philosophy underlying this move was to make every function and work process customer-centric.

Though a customer-centric approach might be the favoured approach of some private enterprises, yet MMTC was used to customers coming to its doorsteps, for getting the materials required, as they had been granted monopoly of some products. Some of MMTC's employees might have developed the attitude of a rationing officer, but that was not to be. Now they were required to go to the customers' doorsteps. This required paradigm shift in attitudes. Fortunately, since many officers were keen to adjust to the new reality, others followed.

Entrepreneurship, Experimentation, and Innovation

Market-led growth required entrepreneurship which was neither consistent with the bureaucratic attitude of a public monopoly nor the audit and vigilance system of the government. Entrepreneurship involved experimentation, trying out new ideas in the market, trial and error, and the possibility of making mistakes and losses in individual transactions. The systems and procedures of public sector undertakings do not tolerate such errors and losses, as they are transaction-driven and not portfolio driven.

To encourage risk taking and entrepreneurship, employees needed assurance that if mistakes were made in experimenting or innovating, they would not be subjected to the vigilance machinery and that the management would support sincere efforts and even bona fide mistakes. The assurance would become credible not because of any statement but because of actual practices. This was successfully achieved in MMTC and it did wonders for the organisation.

Plain dishonesty and lack of integrity was, however, punished. There could have been stray cases of errors of judgement, but every effort was made to make the right decisions. There cannot be any compromise with dishonesty as it destroys an institution. Integrity cannot be taught. Either a person has it or does not have it.

Incapable managers do not necessarily destroy an institution but the dishonest ones never fail to do so.

Improving Cash Flow

The first working capital review revealed that the uncollected trade debtors/sundry debtors (money owed by customers) amounted to Rs. 1713 crore. By this time, the annual turnover had already shrunk by Rs. 5000 crore as compared with the previous year and was soon to fall by another Rs. 1400 crore, thanks to the loss of MMTC monopoly following economic reforms. This was a dangerous situation.

The management concluded that the root causes of this malaise were a faulty credit policy and delegations of powers, false assurance of payment given by one of the ministries to extend credit to the fertilisers manufacturers against post-dated cheques which they failed to back up; obdurate insistence of the government on extending unsecured credit to jewellery exporters for supply of gold without a bank guarantee; unhealthy quality of transactions and faulty risk analysis, extending unsecured credit and acceptance of post-dated cheques.

Preventing trade debts/sundry debtors from becoming non-performing assets

MMTC banned extending unsecured credit and accepting post-dated cheques to prevent further bleeding, revised the delegation of powers to drastically reduce or withdraw the authority to give clean credit without a bank guarantee. It launched a drive to collect sundry debtors through personal visits by the chairman, directors, and the sales team. A directors' committee headed by the chairman met every fortnight for the next five years to review the uncollected debtors, and requested the government to allow to accept bank guarantee against gold loans from the exporter jewellers. But this request was rejected time and again.

MMTC collected most of the old debtors within a year. It started legal proceedings and action by enforcement agencies against defaulters, and wrote off about Rs. 120 crore to clean the balance sheet. An unclean balance sheet is an open invitation to cooking the books and corruption. Recent times have seen major international companies going under due to such non-ethical corporate governance practices. Remember Enron, WorldCom and Satyam? The government had to intervene to save Satyam.

Of the Rs. 1713 crore trade debtors, about Rs. 850 crore was in the shape of post-dated cheques given by major fertiliser companies at the assurance of the fertiliser department. These cheques were dishonoured twice. Legal proceedings were launched against the chairmen and CEOs of all the offending companies. The fertiliser secretary, who was also the chairman of a public sector fertiliser company, agreed to divert fertiliser subsidy (given by the government) to MMTC instead of giving directly to the offending companies. The company succeeded in collecting most of the money locked in dishonoured cheques in this manner and the balance was collected through a barter deal with a PSE by accepting DAP, a fertiliser, manufactured by it, in lieu of the payment due.

This is how sundry debtors were prevented from becoming non-performing assets and money started flowing again in the veins of the company. Determined, sustained, and systemic action was the key to reduce debtors drastically and improve cash flow even in a public sector environment. A business enterprise can choke to death without adequate cash flow.

The company banned extending unsecured credit. It brought to a halt trade in diamonds and to a considerable extent in gold too, which was dependent on extending unsecured credit. It was decided to abandon this part of the diamond business.

However, the gold business was much bigger. MMTC could not afford to stop it. The government insisted on the company giving gold loans to jewellers without bank guarantee. The company made representations against it to the government many times but they were turned down. The ostensible reason given was that such unsecured loans promoted exports by small-scale jewellers. This did result in some jewellers running away with gold and the company chasing them through legal and enforcement agencies. The company and the government had to answer many Parliament questions on this count.

However, a number of other controls in the credit policy were built and a determined drive to collect such debtors was launched which ensured that such non-performing assets did not exceed 0.26% of the total gold business. The government has ultimately allowed MMTC to take bank guarantees against gold loans.

Bringing down inventory levels to healthy norms

The working capital review at MMTC also revealed a high level of inventories amounting to about Rs. 758 crore in 1992. This called for a drastic reduction. Norms of inventory were fixed for each product line and officers were made accountable for adhering to such norms. The Sales and Purchase Committee became more careful so that excess quantity was not ordered. The people who indented the material were made accountable for selling it quickly to avoid unnecessary inventory build-up.

The committee which had been formed to monitor sundry debtors was also made responsible for regularly monitoring inventories and the working capital. Consequently, inventories were brought down considerably. Much of the remaining inventory was due to an obligation imposed by the government to keep buying iron ores from small mines to maintain employment and export later.

These controls helped to improve cash flow and reduced the bank credit and interest burden.

Sharp Definition of the Mission, Clear Priorities, Objectives, and Involvement of All Concerned

The defined mission was *'to emerge as the largest international trader of India for non-oil bulk products and build trade-related infrastructure'*.

The whole organisation was involved in defining the important result areas, fixing targets of volume and profit for each product line, drawing action plans, deciding budget, resource allocation, and effective implementation of the plans/operations. Planning and forecasting was bottoms up and involved a two-way communication. Plans had also to be approved by all the directors and finally by the chairman, who was ultimately accountable to the government. The performance was reviewed against the targets every fortnight and feedback given to the management so that strategies and tactics could be modified depending on market experience.

Introducing uniform formats and compatible information technology systems made it easier to understand comparative performance of branches and divisions and helped finalise the balance sheet much faster. Technology enabled managers to know the order booking, shipments, inventories, and sundry debtors every morning. This enabled the management to take timely action and decisions. Now, of course, an enterprise resource planning (ERP) system has been installed to facilitate the processes.

Shifting Focus from Turnover to Profitability

The management discovered that proper costing of the merchandise was not being done, which undermined profitability. So a simple cost sheet was introduced that invariably included the costs of procurement of products, credit, risk involved, average overheads, contingencies, and the profit margin. Proposals were supposed to be given to the customers based on such a cost sheet and keeping in mind the competition, after getting approval from seniors. Such a cost sheet inculcated money sense in the organisation.

Elimination of Wastage and Avoidable Expenses

Next on radar was wastage and unnecessary expenses. For instance, a regular report on the demurrage paid at the ports was sought. In one year, it was revealed that it amounted to Rs. 17 crore, out of which Rs. 12 crore was to be paid by the company and the balance Rs. 5 crore to be reimbursed by the government on imports done on its behalf. Strict monitoring ensured that almost 90% to 100% demurrage paid was knocked off within two months by properly scheduling the arrival of ships to avoid bunching of vessels, which was responsible for incurring demurrage.

Increasing Productive Expenditure on Customer Creation

While MMTC reduced avoidable expenditure to reduce costs, it increased the expenditure on productive heads like travelling, communications, and customer contact, which helped in increasing business. Companies can seldom be turned around merely by drastic cost reduction across the board. One has to simultaneously increase the income and reduce expenses.

Turning around MITCO

A subsidiary company of MMTC had not only wiped off its equity of about Rs. 8 crore but also another of about Rs. 40 crore. MMTC had to pay staff salary and also meet other expenses.

The management reduced expenditure drastically by closing down a few offices, eliminating wastage and rationalising staff by offering an attractive voluntary retirement scheme. Simultaneously, sales and income increased. As a result, MITCO started making operating profit and the big bleed stopped. Reference was made to BIFR (Board for Industrial and Financial Reconstruction), which advised winding up this subsidiary. However, the government ultimately decided to merge MITCO in MMTC in the interest of maintaining employment.

Concentrating on Three to Four Commanding Heights for Cost Control and Revenue Increase

In business, 20% of events contribute to 80% of the results/profit; and the balance to most of the costs of the company. Therefore, it pays to concentrate on the 20% events. MMTC management followed this rule for both cost control and revenue augmentation by concentrating on three to four items which gave best results. It also saved time and other resources, which could have been wasted on lesser priorities, contributing insignificant results.

In bullion (gold and silver), one of the four priority product lines, the annual revenue increased from about Rs. 475 crore during 1992–1993 to about Rs. 2000 crore during 1996–1997 and the annual trading profit during this period went up from about Rs. 4 crore to about Rs. 42 crore. The dedicated efforts made MMTC the largest trader of bullion in the country.

What Made the Growth in Bullion Business Possible?

An important reason was the brilliant leadership and the creation of many leaders throughout this division who worked with a missionary spirit. A large number of officers and staff worked like people possessed. Many pilots were initiated and then expanded into large businesses. These efforts also touched the entire country and brought MMTC much closer to public through exhibitions of jewellery and retail shops at the international airports and in the domestic tariff area.

The second factor that contributed to the growth was a very simple innovation. Non-resident Indians (NRIs) were allowed at that time to import 5 kilograms of gold at a concessional rate of ad-valorem duty that worked to about 1/13th of the standard rate of duty, which other importers like MMTC had to pay.

The logic to justify the concessional customs duty was that the NRIs paid for the gold in foreign exchange held abroad. These NRIs often offloaded this gold to the Indian jewellers at a profit. Since this gold was much cheaper because of lower duty than that supplied by MMTC, it made a big hole in the company's sales.

A representation was made demanding benefit of concessional rate of customs duty to be available to all the exporters who maintained foreign exchange currency accounts in foreign countries and who used this account to pay for import of gold. Finally, the government conceded to the plea.

As soon as the notification was issued, MMTC ran with success because it had already built a superior infrastructure for gold.

The company had been organising jewellery exhibitions in foreign countries where associate jewellers showcased their products. MMTC decided to hold exhibitions in India using a different business model. Gold was given to jewellers to fabricate jewellery and test its purity in the company's hallmarking and assaying unit before exhibiting the products.

Such certified and hallmarked jewellery would be displayed and sold by MMTC staff drawn from all the branches. The basic concept was that a government company selling hallmarked and certified jewellery would instil much more confidence in the public than private jewellers. This business model proved an instant success. It increased sales and profit margins. The employees at large gathered confidence to sell and make profits.

The first exhibition held at the biggest hall in Delhi drew crowds to such an extent that hardly any walking space was left. The second exhibition, at a huge venue in Mumbai, resulted in queues spilling over to the main road outside the hotel, making it difficult for it to be formally inaugurated. This was a great confidence builder for the staff, paving the way for greater sales not only in the gold division but in other divisions as well.

The success of these domestic jewellery exhibitions paved the way for another enterprise. MMTC set up its own state-of-the-art jewellery shops at international airports and subsequently in the domestic tariff area as well. This is how one business led to another in its adjacency.

Rajesh Khosla was the director who led this division from the front with distinction.

During 2009–10, the turnover of this division exceeded Rs. 29,000 crore and promising joint ventures and other plans are under execution which will lead to further prosperity. Profitability in gold has gone down because of the competition, but hopefully new measures planned like the joint venture for a gold refinery/medallions will restore profitability.

The company needs to think beyond bullion and introduce more innovative schemes like the acceptance of old jewellery from the public in exchange for new; introduce schemes like saving small quantities of gold every year for the marriage of children and issue gold certificates for such savings in gold; promote own brand and sell it through a wide network of franchise holders in India and abroad, and undertake some other schemes after examining the merits and demerits of each proposal.

Fertilisers

MMTC imported urea on behalf of the central government. It was the largest importer of India and the second largest of the world. It continued to retain this status, despite the loss of monopoly in 1995. It also started selling other fertilisers in the domestic market. The import was handled by Rajesh Khosla and the domestic sales by Dr BC Mallik. Later, Dr Mallik handled the import and domestic trade of the fertilisers.

Game-Changing Initiatives of the Minerals Division

In the minerals division, the management concentrated on signing and delivering long-term five-year contracts for iron ore with Japan, South Korea, and others. It also started a determined bid to make aggressive forays into the Chinese market by establishing direct links with the steel mills. This ensured a constant flow of business and profits.

The initiative in China proved very beneficial as this expanded into the largest iron ore business of the company later. Constant efforts have been made to improve the quality of iron ore at the mine heads and improve the infrastructure at the ports and the rail heads to minimise customer complaints, particularly from Japan.

The other major strategic initiative was to establish a joint venture company with the Government of Orissa, Neelachal Ispat Nigam Ltd.

MMTC started receiving national awards for highest exports of minerals every year, starting 1992–93 and this uninterrupted spree continues. The success of this division was due to the excellent leadership provided by SD Kapoor and later by Sanjiv Batra, and the hard work of a large number of experienced and dedicated staff.

Metals continued to be a major business. In the absence of hedging, it was sometimes profitable while at others it was not. But the company continued to hold the largest market share in the import of most non-ferrous metals. Many experiments were made to learn the skills of hedging, but no foolproof solution could be found to the possibility of incurring losses in foreign exchange. Fear of enquiries in such an eventuality prevented officers to hedge, though MMTC secured the government approval to hedge a couple of non-ferrous metals.

Major strides in the trading of commodities like sugar, rice, wheat, and soya bean meal were also made and MMTC emerged the fourth largest agro trader in the country in a short span. About 500,000 tons of sugar was imported in 1995–96.

Trading in hydrocarbons, including coal which became a big business was also undertaken. MMTC's imports of coal/ hydrocarbons in 2007 were over Rs. 1630 crore. During 2008–09, the business exceeded Rs. 3147 crore giving a sizable trading profit of about Rs. 43 crore.

The above strategy and measures helped transform and turn MMTC around

Consolidation and New Initiatives

Continuity in the public sector is a rare luxury and MMTC was blessed in this respect in the sense that initially SD Kapoor and later Sanjiv Batra consolidated the initiatives undertaken. They took many new initiatives too, particularly in the fields of non-conventional energy, power trading, export processing zones, free trade warehousing zones, gem and jewellery SEZ, SEZ for agro commodities, LME warehouse, minting and refining of gold and silver, and setting up commodity exchanges.

The projects which have already been executed include the first phase of NINL, a 1.1 million tons integrated pig iron and steel plant/met coke/power plant in Orissa. The first phase consists of pig iron only. The second phase of this project consisting of steel making facility is expected to be commissioned by December, 2010. The total cost of the first phase of the project was over Rs. 2000 crore and that of the second phase will be about Rs. 1700 crore. Investment of MMTC in the equity of NINL is Rs. 199 crore and its share in the total equity is 49.9%. It is the majority shareholder having management control.

It commissioned a 15 MW wind energy farm in Karnataka at an investment of Rs. 69 crore in 2007.

Projects under implementation include the following:

Phase 2 of NINL, Phase 1 of Ennore Port Project, a commodity exchange, a medallion manufacturing and refining unit, retail jewellery showrooms, currency exchange and coal blocks exploration. The total cost of these projects is about Rs. 2537 crore. MMTC expects to make an investment of about Rs. 370 crore in these projects during 2009/2010.

SICAL Logistics and L&T are the joint venture partners for the iron ore berth at Ennore Port, India Bulls for the Commodity Exchange, PAMP S.A., Switzerland, the largest medallion manufacturer of the world, for the Medallion/Refining Unit, Gitanjali Gems for retailing showrooms, and Jaypee Associates and a few banks for the Currency Exchange, Tata Steel for exploration and exploitation of minerals like iron ore, coal, gold, and diamonds in India and abroad, and Jaypee Securities for the Screen Based Trading project.

A coal block for exploration has been allotted.

Projects under consideration include an iron ore berth at Paradip Port, a coal berth at Paradip Port, an iron ore mining lease and pelletisation plant, coal block in Chattisgarh, and potash mining in Canada.

Direction of MMTC

MMTC's efforts point out the direction in which the company is moving in the future — primarily in building trade-related infrastructure, development of natural resources, and adding value by concentrating on their core competency of bulk handing and diversifying into its adjacencies. Thus, it has ensured continuation of policies consistent with the concept of the company and its core competence, hammered out earlier.

Success in Future

MMTC's success in future will depend upon learning management skills of a large number of joint ventures it has started. It needs to build sufficient controls for the management and skills of dealing with joint venture partners, if they have to reap full benefits of investments. It also needs competent and well-trained managers to man these joint ventures. Development of such new skills is going to be one of the major responsibilities of its management in the future.

The company also needs to increase focus on profitability, trading higher volumes of bulk products, and developing a small number of up-stream and down-stream value chains. Competency in execution and oversight are the quintessential skills. Without them, the best of the plans will merely remain honest intentions. The company would considerably benefit from training its people for these skills and acquiring them. However, MMTC is moving in the right direction, and largely confining itself to the concept of the company, core competency and its adjacencies.

After some time, MMTC may have to examine if the assumptions of its business are still valid and whether they need to be replaced by more valid assumptions.

Business Results

Market cap of MMTC

The Economic Times, dated April 3, 2008, carried a front page story, hailing MMTC as the new *Midas toucher* and the second biggest wealth producer of the country during that particular year. MMTC, by and large, ranked amongst the top 5/6 public and private sector companies on the basis of market cap during 2008–2009. However, it ranked third in the market cap on October 14, 2009, in the same publication's report on October

15, 2009. Only two other companies, Reliance Industries and ONGC had a higher market cap on that day. The *Mint* reported that the *market cap of MMTC on that day was Rs. 1,77,062 crore*, although its equity was only Rs. 50 crore. MMTC'S scrip of the face value of Rs. 10 was quoted on the Bombay Stock Exchange at Rs. 35,412 on that day. The P/E ratio was 1157.65, one of the best in the country.

At present, a very small percentage of its equity has been disinvested. It is expected that the price of its scrip may be adjusted downwards after a larger percentage of its shares are disinvested. Even after accounting for this possibility, the performance of its scrip has been impressive by all accounts. MMTC is one of the PSEs, which will have to disinvest up to 10% of its equity, according to a recent decision of the government. However, before this happens, the value of its Rs. 10 scrip may have to be reduced to a smaller denomination and the government. may be tempted to demand attractive bonus shares.

Business turnover

The annual turnover of MMTC touched Rs. 26,423 crore in 2007–08. It exceeded Rs. 36,500 crore during 2008–2009 and is expected to exceed Rs. 45,000 crore during 2009–2010 despite the global recession.

The company has indeed come a long way from the days when it was widely feared that it might have to shut shop after the economic reforms of 1991.

Subsidiaries

MTPL, the subsidiary set up at Singapore, with an equity contribution by MMTC of only US$1 million, contributed an annual turnover of about US$687 million during 2008–09. This subsidiary, which has only about 13 employees, has contributed profit after a tax of US$6.8 million during the same year. Its profit is expected to be over Rs. 32 crore during 2009–2010. The net worth of MTPL during 2008–09 was US$15 million. The dividend given to MMTC is much more than what it had originally invested. This is a shining example of how well the public sector can perform if the companies are made autonomous. If the government too develops hands-off approach adopted by MMTC in case of this subsidiary, most PSEs would do well.

NINL, a joint venture for pig iron and steel, contributed to MMTC a turnover of about Rs. 1475 crore during 2007–08. This plant, which is spread over an area of about 2500 hectares and has been allotted captive iron ore mines, is up and running and giving healthy profits. During 2007–08, it turned in a profit of Rs. 120 crore.

The captive iron ore mines allotted to its steel plant, having iron ore reserves of about 110 million tons, represent a lot of wealth. This joint venture is also a source of profit to MMTC on a perennial basis, as it has secured the rights to be its sole selling and purchase agents. NINL is also a dependable source of new products and by-products made by these plants. MMTC has already earned a decent profit from NINL that has more than justified its investment in the latter.

The office complex, built in Bandra Kurla complex in Mumbai, commands a premium of more than Rs. 1000 crore.

MMTC is the largest importer of bullion and non-ferrous metals, the largest exporter of minerals like iron ore, chrome ore and manganese ore and a leading international trader of agro commodities like fertilisers, wheat, rice, sugar, and pulses, and other bulk products like coal and hydrocarbons. It is the biggest international trader of India for non-oil bulk products. It is integrating backwards and forwards to develop linkages from mines to markets.

It has very valuable assets in the steel plant, met coke plant, power plant, captive mines, other joint ventures and subsidiaries, office buildings and housing complexes, etc.

Shoulders of Worthy Predecessors

MMTC had the good fortune to be chaired by many distinguished persons who built it brick by brick since its inception in 1963. They included luminaries like M/S Govind Narain, ICS; TP Singh, ICS; RR Bahl, ICS; S Ramchandran; CR Das; CR Swaminathan; DK Dhaon; SVS Raghavan; SK Agarwal; and IP Hazarika. In addition, a few distinguished persons officiated as CMDs for brief spells. Many distinguished persons served on the board and made remarkable contributions to the company.

It has been built on the shoulders of its preceding officials, as was the case with this incumbent and his successors: SD Kapoor and Sanjiv Batra.

The progress of an organisation depends on the quality of leadership it can develop amongst a large section of its employees.

The present board is chaired by Sanjiv Batra, an IIT engineer (due to retire in Sep 2010). He is ably assisted by a coherent and constructive board of full-time directors including HS Mann and Sunir Khurana (marketing directors). They are doing a splendid job. AR Goyal, A Mahapatra and SK Kar retired recently after making a significant contribution to the company. Ved Prakash has joined as a marketing director.

The whole-time directors who extended unstinted support to the new initiatives between 1992 and 1997 were SK Kumar, SR Mehta, Dr BBL Madhukar, Dr BC Mallik, SD Kapoor, Rajesh Khosla and PN Sharma. Dr Madhukar also acted as the chairman and managing director for nine months after I retired.

The constructive role played by the unions and officers associations is an important factor in the turnaround of the company. They accepted many changes with grace and worked shoulder to shoulder with the rest of the organisation under very trying conditions. They sincerely tried to adopt new attitudes and working habits, which were more customer- and market-oriented.

SOFTWARE OF THE TRANSFORMATION

Grim Battle for Survival between 1992 and 1997

MMTC was fighting a life and death battle in 1992. However, it was blessed as there had been a few brave souls who had the fire in their belly and the grit and determination to turn the tide. They and the teams they inspired changed the course of the company. The senior management tried to remove obstacles in their way and functioned as an enabler so that they could run fast without stumbling. Those who stumbled were sure to find support and a helping hand.

The mission, core competency, and the concept of the company were defined sharply. Strategy, targets, and plans were derived from them. Focussing on commanding heights in both cost control and revenue increase brought about maximum economy and revenue maximisation. Top priority was given to control sundry debtors of over Rs. 1700 crore and an inventory of about Rs. 750 crore, which improved cash flow, reduced interest cost, and inculcated money sense.

The turnover, including that of MTPL, increased to Rs. 6600 crore within four years from the rump turnover of Rs. 1500 crore left in 1992, out of which another Rs. 400 crore worth of business that was producing bad debts instead of profit, was voluntarily abandoned. It will be much higher at today's prices. Average profit per year during 1992-97 was over Rs. 50 crore despite 80% fall in the income. The company took off after this and the recent results have already been mentioned.

The customer was made the main focus of the company.

Maximum stress was placed on execution of plans. People who showed skills in execution were given higher responsibility, challenging assignments, better promotions, and shown more respect by the senior management. They were projected as role models.

All communication meetings were steered to take decisions, assign responsibility for execution, and ensure that previous decisions were executed. The management tried to ask the right questions instead of giving the right answers to the wrong questions. Failure to ask right questions at the right time can and does lead to management disasters or lacklustre performance. Therefore, raising the right questions at the right time is the prime responsibility of the management and more particularly, of the top management.

At the heart of the turnaround of MMTC were hundreds of scheduled and unscheduled communication meetings.

Diversification versus Pursuit of the Core Competency

A lot of mulling over this dilemma was done and the conclusion drawn that it is not unrelated diversification that pays — it is dogged pursuit of the core competency and investments on it that enables companies to succeed. If one must diversify, the best way is to look for areas contiguous to one's core competency. For example, diversification into trade-related infrastructure, coal, pig iron/steel/met coke, gold medallions, and jewellery retailing was undertaken, which were areas adjacent to core competency.

Diversification

Diversification in contiguous areas kept the company within the broad confines of core competence of bulk handling and the overall concept.

There are some exceptions to this general guideline and some companies have managed to diversify successfully in unrelated fields too. However, it pays to stick to one's knitting or diversify in adjacencies.

Value addition

Value addition provides another opportunity for successful diversification. For instance, the pig iron/steel project was the logical next step in the value addition chain of iron ore, and medallions and jewellery shops added value to gold.

Module-by-Module Approach

The company progressed module-by-module for innovations and new ventures. It is best to make small investments in new ideas at the initial stage and gradually expand the module to bigger investments and businesses. The management made entrepreneurship, innovation, and piloting projects a religion and encouraged people to experiment even at the cost of making mistakes.

Finally, pains were taken to carry along the board of directors, ministers, senior bureaucrats, and most of all our own officers, staff and unions. Drawing on all the sources of cooperation was an important reason for the turnaround.

Walking the Talk

The practices and beliefs propagated by the senior management were actually practised by most. It is only then that people adopt the cultural practices and work habits being advocated. Self-example set by the seniors is the most crucial factor. Wherever there was a divergence between preaching and practice, there were problems.

Changing culture involving old working habits and mindsets is a slow process. People will change if they see an advantage for themselves. The management was at pains to tell people how they would benefit by inculcating new habits and culture.

Ground Realities

Open and frequent communication sessions ensured that whatever we thought, planned, or did was grounded in the reality of the market and the strengths and weaknesses of the people. The ground realities assumed the biggest importance. When frank dialogues are exchanged amongst colleagues keeping in mind the ground realities, the outcomes and decisions are practical. Open communication ensured transparency in decisions, kept everybody informed, and they knew what help is required from them

Appreciation of the ground realities and the current context and making and executing practical policies and strategies based on them was the single most important reason of the metamorphosis of MMTC. Frequent communication was the medium through which we understood and explained the ground realities. Another important factor that ensured good results was choosing our priorities carefully. This actually involved confining to core competency and selecting very few priorities.

Both MMTC and PEC are public sector enterprises, but their government ownership did not come in the way of turning them around. However, they would have fared even better if the reforms of the public sector had been done.

The story of MMTC is one of victory of the human spirit, courage, and hope in the face of a grim battle for survival.

It brings out the human factors of head and heart, which motivate the people to achieve the best they are capable of.

It is a story of how one lamp lit another, and how leadership developed through the length and breadth of the company, which lifted it from its nadir to its zenith. It is a story of courage, grit and determination of the people who were shipwrecked but swam back to safety, only to become stronger and bolder for undertaking a new voyage of exploration.

The story of MMTC, PEC and NINL would not have been so bright had it not been for the extraordinary leadership of Pranab Mukherjee and P Chidambaram, the commerce ministers during my time and their very capable successors. Late AN Verma and Tajinder Khanna, the then commerce secretaries and their successors provided rock-solid support to the new initiatives.

5

The Story of Neelachal Ispat Nigam Ltd.

WHILE THE EARLIER TWO STORIES ABOUT PEC AND MMTC were concerned with what can be achieved *within* the present policies and procedures, the story of NINL is about what can be achieved by *stretching* these policies with the active cooperation of the government. While in both the cases, it was working within the present policies, releasing the power of 'stretch' helped establish a major pig iron/steel plant.

Proposal of a Joint Venture for Making Steel

While hobnobbing in MMTC with the possibility of establishing joint ventures, we were approached by the Government of Orissa to establish a steel plant in collaboration with a local businessman. It wanted the management control with the entrepreneur, while the major investment was to be made by the company for which it would give us the marketing rights.

It was, however, felt that while there was nothing wrong with the entrepreneur, a major integrated steel project might be beyond his financial and administrative muscle, and it might be unsafe to invest in this venture.

During a meeting with the decision makers of the state government, it was conveyed that MMTC could invest only if it had the management control of the project. It was also pointed out that the rate of return on the capital employed was not attractive enough, and hence extra benefits in taxes like the sales tax and excise duty exemptions, etc. for a longer period of 10/15 years than the normal 5/7 years were necessary. This proposal was not accepted by the state government.

Thereafter, the project went into hibernation for more than a year. But when the new government assumed office, it expressed interest in reviving the project.

A meeting was chaired by the Chief Minister in Bhubaneswar which was attended by the ministers of industry, power, mines, finance, revenue, forests and environment, and the secretaries to the state government of these departments, chief secretary, the chairmen of the Pollution Control Board and the Electricity Board and the MMTC team. This meeting acted like a single window clearance in principle for a 1.1 million ton pig iron/steel/met coke/power project and other approvals required from the state government.

Securing Commitments

During this meeting, MMTC sought management control of the project with the state as a partner in the joint venture, the price of land being part of the state's share of equity in addition to their normal equity in cash. It also requested that the chairman of the Pollution Board provide a clearance in principle from an environmental angle, the details being processed subsequently;

the chairman of the Electricity Board to grant in principle permit to install a captive power plant and allow use of the power load from the Electricity Board as a secondary source; and a good mine of iron ore to be allotted on priority for captive use. This was in addition to the assistance requested in procuring about 2500 acres of land in the state.

The Chief Minister suggested that since their state was surplus in power, there was no need for investment in a captive power plant. But being apprehensive about the quality of power, and the possibility of it becoming a power deficit state in the future, which it actually did after some time, we insisted that the approval in principle for setting up a captive power plant be granted while the power from the Electricity Board would serve as a secondary source.

The purpose of the meeting was to ensure that various departments did not drag their feet later when the formal applications for various approvals were submitted.

The idea behind inviting the state government to become a joint venture partner was to have a powerful ally for securing approvals.

The purpose of converting the land price into equity was to reduce MMTC's investment in a major project.

Since all terms to set up this project in Orissa had been accepted, the only thing that remained was the Central Government's approval, which we suspected was almost impossible to secure.

MMTC did not press for extending the extra taxation benefits for a longer period than their normal scheme as others, like Tata Iron and Steel Company Ltd. (TISCO), having bigger footprint in the steel industry and planning a bigger steel plant in the state, would have objected.

THE ODDS AGAINST THE PROJECT

1. Since the steel industry was facing a recession, why embark on it when no one else was doing so?
2. The government was not permitting even a PSE like SAIL to set up Greenfield steel projects, and the chances of their being allowed were dim.
3. MMTC did not have a manufacturing experience.

After giving a serious thought to these issues, and considering the risks involved, it was concluded that:

1. It is better to commence a long gestation steel project during recession so that it is ready by the beginning of the boom.
2. The government will have to revise its policy of not permitting Greenfield pig iron/steel capacity in the public sector to cope with the ever-increasing demands of our infrastructure, automobile and manufacturing industry. With past experience of similar nature, one felt confident of persuading the government to that line of thinking.
3. Retired steel experts from SAIL, TISCO, and other steel plants will be hired to establish and run the operations as was being done by the private steel companies, and supporting them with inputs of an entrepreneur.

Value addition to the iron ore traded by MMTC was 10–12 times. There was a possibility of getting iron ore mines for captive consumption, which meant considerable wealth and a hedge against losing monopoly on export of iron ore, and gaining a monopoly on the sale and purchase of the products manufactured and the raw materials and inputs required, which would boost the turnover and profits. This would give an opportunity to own valuable assets. These were huge opportunities for a trading company.

Considering that MMTC was at an infraction point at this juncture of its history, all it needed was to pursue course-changing strategic initiatives like this project and not just incremental ones. Therefore, it was decided to take the plunge and do whatever was necessary to mitigate risks. The decision involved courage and the officers decided to bet their careers on it.

Selling Concept to the Critical Group

It was vital to enlist the support of the critical decision-making group within the Commerce Ministry including Pranab Mukherjee, the then Union Minister of Commerce; P Chidambaram, the former Commerce Minister who later became the Union Finance Minister; Tajinder Khanna, the then Commerce Secretary who later became the LG of Delhi; and the government directors on the MMTC Board. Their unstinted support pumped in the adrenalin to go ahead full throttle.

Developing the Core Team for the Project

The first job was to form a core group within MMTC.

Asiad Chief Executive Club

I was a member of the Asiad Chief Executive Club (ACE). It was a small but unique group. The members were chairmen and managing directors of major public sector companies, who lived in the Asiad Village in Delhi. They met on rotation every month for dinner. One of the members was Dr SR Jain, Chairman and Managing Director of SAIL. He had worked earlier as the CMD of Coal India Ltd. and HEC Ltd. At an appropriate time during one of these dinners, a proposal was made to him to get associated with the organisation as an advisor after his impending retirement. He was gracious enough to accept the proposal, though he knew he would get more lucrative offers from others. This was the best thing that could have happened to the project. Incidentally, this story also brings out the power of building informal professional social networks.

Dr Jain was requested to recruit capable steel experts from a pool of retired officers who had worked with him in SAIL, experts from TISCO and other steel companies. At the top of his agenda had to be his recommendation to the board for the recruitment of a managing director for this project. He proposed Dr Subroto Ray for this post.

One has already narrated the story of how Dr Subroto Ray, the former managing director of the Bhilai Steel Plant, was recruited as managing director of the steel project within half an hour. Between Dr Jain and Subroto and some assistance from MMTC, they soon completed the core team of steel experts, most of whom had worked with them earlier.

Within MMTC, one of the directors, SD Kapoor, a metallurgical engineer who had earlier worked in SAIL for a few years in the marketing department, was presently in charge of the mineral division exporting iron ore and other minerals. He was given the responsibility of this project as well. A small nucleus of three or four other officers assisted him.

This completed the initial core team for the steel project within MMTC and was the first building block of this project.

Neelachal Ispat Nigam Ltd.

The people of Orissa and other Hindus have deep faith in Lord Neelachal who is Lord Vishnu. Since the project was situated in Orissa, it was decided to name it as 'Neelachal

Ispat Nigam Ltd.' and the captive 800,000 tons pa metallurgical Coke Company as 'Konarak Met Coke Ltd. (KMCL), after the famous Konarak Sun temple.

Naming the new company after the most venerated deity of Orissa ensured not only blessings of the almighty but also those of the mighty officials of the state government. It also endeared the company to the populace and facilitated in procuring land for establishing the steel plant.

Later, KMCL was merged with Neelachal Ispat Nigam Ltd. along with the 62.5 MW capacity captive power plant.

The Woman, the Child, and the Steel Plant

MMTC bought iron ore for exports. One day, while touring the iron ore areas, one came across labourer women carrying iron ore buckets on their heads, with babies on their backs under the blazing sun when the mercury was touching 46 degree centigrade.

The mothers were sweating under the weight and the children crying themselves hoarse under the fury of the sun. Their abject poverty strengthened the resolve to establish a steel plant near the iron ore mines to improve the living conditions of at least some of these poor people.

Making Suppliers and Project Consultants Equity Partners

MECON prepared a detailed project report (DPR) for a fee of Rs. 5 crore. This was eventually converted into equity just as the state government had done for the cost of land. This ensured effective cooperation of both. MECON had to bet their fee on their recommendations to make the management more confident.

This model was repeated later too when MMTC persuaded equipment suppliers like BHEL, BECO, SMS, and Danieli to become minor equity partners. NMDC, the supplier of Bailadila iron ore also chipped in with an equity of Rs. 49 crore. This was over and above the state government converting the price of land amounting to about Rs. 25 crore into equity, in addition to cash contribution to the equity by IPICOL and OMC.

According to a company publication of NINL of February, 2008, MMTC with its equity contribution of Rs. 199 crore held 49.78% of the total equity, the Government of Orissa 26.29% through IPICOL and OMC, NMDC 12.26%, MECON 1.25%, BHEL 1.25%, other equipment suppliers 1.91%, and FIs and Banks 7.27%. The total equity was Rs. 399.8 crore. The debt portion in the first phase of the project was Rs. 1449 crore.

Procurement of Land

About 2500 acres of land was allotted at Duburi in Jajpur district. Dr Subroto Ray and his team ensured possession. Considering the problems faced for procuring land by the Tatas in Nandigram for the Nano small car project and in Duburi right opposite the Kalinga Nagar plant, and POSCO of South Korea for their proposed 12 million tons steel project, the company was fortunate in acquiring much larger area. This was partly because the issue was less politicised by then and partly due to the tact and sincerity of Dr Ray's team that offered a fair deal to the land owners.

Seeking Simultaneous Approvals

One of the reasons why the public sector and government projects face inordinate delays and cost overruns is that many of them do not move simultaneously on all fronts. In this case, it was decided to acquire all approvals simultaneously for land, water, power, environment, mining leases and prospecting licences, etc., from the state and central government, notwithstanding the fact that there was no formal approval of the Project Investment Board (PIB), though there was the approval of the administrative ministry. Consequently, it was firing on all the engines simultaneously. This simple technique helped save a colossal amount of time and cost overruns.

The Story of the Blast Furnace

The company was offered a second hand ILVA blast furnace in Italy. The management decided to explore this possibility to reduce the capital cost of the project. A team of technical experts comprising Dr SR Jain; SD Kapoor; Kulkarni of MECON; Dr Mohanty, who was the Managing Director of Orissa Sponge Iron India Ltd. and had originally brought this proposal; and PM Mahapatra, who later succeeded RN Das as the Chief Secretary of Orissa; visited Italy to assess the condition of the blast furnace. They also visited Mexico to assess alternative possibilities of buying second hand blast furnace. This technical team recommended buying the second hand blast furnace from ILVA, Italy.

The question was how to buy it without formal approval of the PIB for the main project itself, for which neither the administrative ministry nor the company had yet applied.

As a first step, the board of directors was approached for permission to buy the furnace, emphasising that the opportunity of reducing steeply the project cost should not be lost, as the furnace was reported by the expert team to be in very good condition. The time for buying was short, and an urgent decision was required.

CM Vasudev, the joint secretary of the ministry of commerce and the government nominee on the board was similarly convinced. But the second government nominee on the board, Ajit Kumar, additional secretary and financial advisor, disagreed. His objection was more philosophical, and he opined that the blast furnace would simply 'rot and rust' as there was no continuity of the chairman and managing director in the public sector.

Since the opinion of the board was 7:1 in favour of the import, Ajit Kumar requested that his dissent be recorded in the minutes, which was promptly done. There was lot of weight in what Ajit Kumar said but he underestimated what determination, human spirit, team work, and continuity of similar thinking that comes through a willing coalition of minds, could achieve even in the public sector.

The Minister of Commerce, Pranab Mukherjee, the wise and the far-sighted statesman that he is, wasted no time in granting the approval on the basis of the board's recommendations. The support of Tajinder Khanna, the then Commerce Secretary and CM Vasudev was an added advantage.

Once all the approvals were in order, the blast furnace under zero customs duty scheme offering an export obligation was imported. Little time was wasted to remove the huge equipment from an Indian port to claim the zero duty benefit by a certain date. A team led by the general manager was put in charge of this operation. Various parts of the furnace were to be transported in trucks and trailers to the project site, Duburi. But a peculiar problem arose.

Removing Road Blocks

The transmission towers on the highway blocked the movement of excessively high parts of the blast furnace and the failure to overcome the problem within the next couple of days would have resulted in the loss of zero customs duty benefit. But the general manager and his team managed to get an approval to remove the transmission towers, move the trucks and trailers on this road overnight, and then reinstall them in their original location within a day.

The blast furnace at Duburi was stored close to the site of the project before it could be installed after refurbishing it with new electric items and latest automation.

The Tale of Funding the Steel Project

A credit of about Rs. 1000 crore (later increased to Rs. 1449 crore) was needed from the financial institutions and banks to fund the project besides the equity contribution of the partners. Despite the best efforts, the application to the IDBI, the leading financial institution of the consortium was initially rejected outright because it was felt MMTC was an international trading company having no experience of manufacturing. Therefore, the risk of lending to such a company was not advisable.

It was brought to the notice of the Chairman of IDBI that MMTC was not going to manufacture steel. This was the job of a new company, Neelachal Ispat Nigam Ltd., which was a joint venture of MMTC, the Government of Orissa, MECON, and possibly some private partners who might join later. Retired or serving experts from the Steel Authority of India, TISCO, and other private steel plants were going to build and run this plant.

Further, it was submitted that even private industrialists recruited experts from the public sector and that they had built fortunes based on their experience. So why a public sector company like MMTC could not do it?

It was also argued that the role of MMTC would be that of an entrepreneur who supplied leadership, seeding capital, overall supervision and assistance, and ensured that experts were recruited to set up and run the project.

His other objection was that setting up green field steel projects in the public sector was banned by the Government of India and even the Steel Authority of India was not permitted to do so. Therefore, he could not fund us. This was indeed a deadly objection.

It was pointed out that the above decision was based on an outdated assessment of demand and supply and a misplaced philosophical belief that the public sector should not set up green field steel plants as it was not in the public interest. To equate public interest with the private sector only was a flavour of the season, and in due course, the government would change this thinking as the demands of the infrastructure, construction, automobiles and other sectors become overwhelming. It took a long time to develop a steel project. Therefore, it was in the national interest to fund such a project right away so that the country was well prepared to meet the additional demand created by the infrastructure and construction needs, without loss of time.

His next objection was that the steel industry was not doing well and was in recession and that the IDBI had already overexposed itself to the steel industry. Therefore, it would be dangerous to fund yet another pig iron and steel project.

It was argued that the steel industry was cyclical. It had its troughs and peaks and perhaps it had entered the trough phase at this time and hence this pessimism and that itself was a good enough reason to fund it now so that it could start production in the peak of the steel cycle since it took a long time to plan and establish a steel plant. Therefore, it would pay them to lend to such a project in a trough period.

Besides, MMTC had a reliable project consultant like MECON that had prepared a detailed project report and was very confident about profitability and capacity to return the loans.

Finally, it was emphasised that at least a team of their experts could be deputed to do a Due Diligence exercise to establish or reject the veracity of MECON's claims.

However, the chairman of IDBI stood his ground despite all the arguments advanced and refused to fund our project.

Help from unexpected quarters

The outcome of this disappointing meeting was communicated to a senior financial official in the government with the conviction that the project was in the national interest, and that the IDBI should fund this project. And that was the end of it or so it seemed until on a second visit, the Chairman of IDBI was found to be a different person and keen to fund the project. He ordered his team to start the Due Diligence exercise.

The Due Diligence team was suitably impressed and recommended a funding of about Rs. 1000 crore from IDBI, other financial institutions and the commercial banks, which were part of the consortium to lend money. The team at the steel plant, the Finance Director and the core team played their part well in convincing the consortium members. The funding was granted.

This was followed by getting other approvals like land, water, electricity and environment clearance.

The idea behind narrating the story is to show that major hurdles, which look seemingly impossible, can be overcome even in a public sector setting.

Roping in the private sector

The next step was an attempt to involve TISCO, which had the reputation of running companies in a professional manner and on ethical lines.

KC Mehra, a member of the TISCO board of directors was approached. He was enthusiastic and suggested setting up a meeting with the full board of TISCO at Kolkata, minus JJ Irani, the managing director. It was conveyed that MMTC was keen to obtain TISCO's co-operation in setting up and running this plant in return for which a management fee and a share in the equity, if desired, will be given. However, Irshad Hussain, the finance director, who acted as their chief spokesman, said that they were already overcommitted in their investments and did not have the funds or the spare management resources. TISCO refused.

POSCO, which is now trying to set up a 12 million tons steel project in Orissa, also declined a partnership offer. It has been struggling since 2005 to acquire land and mining lease for iron ore for their project but without success because of the resistance of the farmers and other ginger groups. Had it accepted the MMTC offer, 2500 acres would have been on the platter, along with a captive mining lease for iron ore.

A similar offer was made to Nippon Steel of Japan. But it too passed on the buck to its trading companies.

Finally, the Commonwealth Development Corporation (CDC) and Lucky Gold Star of South Korea agreed to invest in the equity. However, as the recession in the steel industry deepened, it too changed tracks subsequently.

But MMTC had in place the land and other approvals of the state government, a second-hand blast furnace under erection after refurbishing, a managing director of the newly formed joint venture company and a team of steel experts.

Specifications were notified for various equipment requirements for Phase 1 of the project. Tenders and enquiries were floated for the purchase of various packages of equipment, civil construction, fabrication and auxiliaries, etc., not only for

NINL but also for KMCL and the power plant. Work on the boundary wall, civil works, and blast furnace refurbishing and other plants started in right earnest. Packages involving long delivery time were ordered earlier than the shorter delivery packages to save time.

By this time, about Rs. 70 crore had already been invested with the approval of the ministry. But the formal approval of the PIB was nowhere in sight.

In the mid-1990s, there were no *Navratnas* and *Mini Ratnas* having automatic powers to invest and all MOU signing PSEs had to seek approval of the PIB for making investments in the projects. This involved a time-consuming scrutiny by many ministries and the planning commission, before being finally considered by the PIB.

The Project Investment Board

Finally, when the PIB was formally approached by our administrative ministry, some ministries and the planning commission dragged their feet. They grumbled that they had been brought in the loop too late by our ministry. They showed reluctance to approve investment in this project. This was a big setback.

Change of Government Brings New Worries

In the meantime, new worries overwhelmed. The government changed. The new political set up ordered presentation after presentation of NINL without coming to any conclusion.

However, the bureaucracy within the ministry continued to lend staunch support to the project. The support received from DP Bagchi, additional secretary and FA and board director deserves special mention. Bagchi later rose to become the chief secretary of Orissa and supported this project whole-heartedly in his new capacity too.

The new political order in the ministry did not see eye to eye and shot down the US$3 billion project for setting up a major port in Orissa on which already Rs. 1 crore had been invested just for getting a detailed project report ready. SAIL, TISCO, Larsen & Toubro, one of the public sector petroleum companies, and the Government of Orissa had agreed in principle to collaborate with MMTC in the joint venture and become equity partners and the major captive users of the port. A major port project on the eastern coast of India in collaboration with such renowned companies and captive users and future customers like the major steel plants coming up in Orissa like those of POSCO of Korea and Arcelor Mittal, would have been a great asset for the nation and the company.

It was feared that the pig iron and steel project would meet the same fate and the investment made would be wasted.

SOS to the Prime Minister

With the help of the Orissa Chief Minister in 1997, the company approached the prime minister, HD Deve Gowda, with the information that an investment of Rs. 70 crore had already been made in the integrated pig iron, steel, met coke and power complex that were already at an advanced stage of construction. And if the investment was to be rescued, approval of the Government of India was needed expeditiously.

The Prime Minister was convinced and convened a Cabinet meeting to consider this project. Normally, only the PIB considers such proposals. An exception was made in this case.

A meeting was also sought with P Chidambaram, the then union finance minister, who supported the project earlier as the commerce minister.

Chidambaram felt that the management control of such a project should ideally be transferred to the private sector. He was duly briefed that the Commonwealth Development Corporation, UK and Lucky Gold Star, South Korea, had agreed to invest in the equity as private sector partners, as our efforts to rope in TISCO, POSCO and Nippon Steel had not succeeded. It was suggested that the company be allowed to establish this project in the public sector, and once the private equity players took a stake, there would be scope for transferring the management control to the private sector partners.

What MMTC wanted out of this joint venture as a trading company was the right to sell the products and by-products, both in the domestic and export markets, import all their inputs, and sell some other raw materials to them. Such selling and buying rights were expected to add over Rs. 2000 crore per annum to the top line and about Rs. 60–80 crore per annum to the bottom line as commission/service charges on pig iron production alone. Both the top and the bottom line would improve further after the steel production commenced.

It was not possible to secure these rights without management control. Hence, it was important to retain management control at least till the selling and buying rights were secured through legally enforceable agreements with NINL. After the trading rights were secured through legal contracts with NINL, even privatisation would not have seriously disturbed the main motive of setting up this joint venture.

The Last Post

The central Cabinet approved an equity contribution by MMTC of Rs. 100 crore for the pig iron/steel plant (NINL), Rs. 50 crore for the captive KMCL and the Power Plant, thanks to the support given by the prime minister and Chidambaram.

MMTC still continues to retain the management control of NINL and is making handsome profits. Unfortunately, the private parties, who had agreed to partner, disappeared in thin air, as the trough of the steel trade cycle deepened. But MMTC saw it through till it commenced production and started making profits.

It is now being speculated that the UPA Government is now mulling the sale of NINL to either SAIL or RINL, both PSEs, perhaps because the steel industry is consolidating throughout the world. If this happens, MMTC is likely to make a huge profit on the sale of its shares and still retain the selling and buying rights for perpetuity, as per legally binding agreements between MMTC and NINL. NINL also has the choice to float its own Initial Public Offering (IPO) to raise funds for further expansion. It seems to keep its options open for the present.

On retirement, soon after the Cabinet's approval of the pig iron/steel project, I bade goodbye as the chairman of MMTC, rather than accepting an extension of seven months,

The production of pig iron commenced soon after the construction of the plant.

The flag was carried by SD Kapoor who became the full-time chairman and managing director after a gap of about a year during which time there were two officiating chairmen. Dr SR Jain continued to advise the steel project and still does. Dr Subroto Ray delivered the goods expected of him. Unfortunately, Subroto died suddenly in harness. He worked as a committed man till his last day.

Later, MMTC's equity stake was raised to Rs. 199 crore with the approval of the government. The plant is in operation and manufactures over 0.6 million tons of pig iron. PC Sahu is the Managing Director of NINL.

The cooperation extended by the Government of Orissa has proved most valuable in not only becoming the second biggest equity partner, but also in giving timely help at all stages. The political executives and bureaucrats of the state and the chairmen of IPICOL and OMC have extended exemplary support.

In the first phase of the integrated pig iron/steel plant which has been set up with an investment of about Rs. 2000 crore, the company is manufacturing pig iron and blast furnace (BF) coke as the main products. The excess BF coke and the by-products generated like granulated slag, crude tar, ammonium sulphate, nut coke, coke breeze, and CI scrap are sold in the open market to improve the profitability of NINL.

NINL, in 2009, was the largest producer and exporter of pig iron in the country. It is having its own captive power plant of 62.5 MW. Further, it is exporting its excess power to GRIDCO, a unit of the Government of Orissa, and is entitled to earn carbon credits on some of their projects as their commitment to clean environment.

The annual turnover of NINL was about Rs. 1474 crore during 2007–08.

Work on Phase 2 of the project, consisting of steel making facilities, is in full swing at an investment of about Rs. 1683 crore and is likely to be completed by 2010. The products under the steel melting shop, which is under construction, are billets, bars and wire rods. The construction work on the steel melting shop, billet caster, bars and rod mill has already started. After this, the project will achieve a full production of 1.1 million tons per annum.

Expansion Plans

NINL is having its own captive mines for iron ore at Koira in Sundergarh and Keonjhar district of Orissa in an area of

1800 hectares. It has estimated reserves of about 110 million tons of iron ore. NINL plans to develop a 2 million tons per annum mechanised mine on a two-shift operation basis to meet its requirement of iron ore on a sustainable and long-term basis. This will further improve the economics of NINL.

NINL had made a net profit of about Rs. 120 crore in 2007–08 and about Rs. 58 crore in 2006–07, according to a company release.

All the facts and figures given are based on the company releases, balance sheets, and discussion with senior officers of the company.

NINL has enabled a trading company like MMTC to get into trading of many new products including basic and foundry grade pig iron, granulated slag, coking coal, coke, nut and breeze coke, crude tar and ammonium sulphate and power trading, and raw materials like lime stone and dolomite, etc. Once steel production is added, MMTC shall also have products like steel billets, steel wire rods and bars, etc.

NINL made handsome profits right from the initial year of its production. MMTC too has already earned more than Rs. 500 crore towards its sales and purchase commission on either the products or supply of inputs to it during the last 10 years besides dividends.

Unique Features

NINL was set up in the public sector despite the then policy of the Government of India not to establish any green field steel project in the public sector.

The financial institutions and banks financed it to the tune of more than Rs. 1000 crore, despite a policy of not funding such projects in a recessionary phase of the steel industry to which they were already overexposed.

This is the first steel company to give a profit (Rs. 108 crore) right in the first full year of its commercial production.

The company has always paid back its instalments of interest on its loans right on time. Not many steel companies have such a record.

It was the first steel plant promoted by an international trading company in the public sector which had no prior experience and expertise of manufacturing pig iron and steel. This was the first steel plant in the country linked with a trading company that assumed the responsibility of sales and purchase for most of its products and inputs.

It had a unique management model. It was conceived and financed by a public sector company and was manned by the retired and other officers of the public sector. There were no business tycoons to promote it and no budgetary support was taken from the government either. Even the steel plants established by SAIL were started with budgetary support from the government.

The board of directors of NINL consisting of full-time directors of MMTC and representatives of the Government of Orissa, etc. did not interfere with the day-to-day working of the company, leaving the details to the steel experts. *This hands-off approach was unique for the promoters in the public sector.*

This project was conceived, planned, and executed during the trough period of the steel industry cycle when no steel entrepreneurs in India were daring to establish new capacity. Consequently, the plant was ready by the time the peak of the trade cycle approached and started making profit from day one.

It was a bold experiment. No other public sector undertaking had been allowed to establish this kind of a venture without the prior approval of the PIB of the Government of India.

This was the only project which was considered and approved straight by the Cabinet of the Union Government even without the approval of the PIB, permitting it to invest Rs. 150 crore in the equity of the joint venture, which was later increased to Rs. 199 crore.

The number of men employed per ton of production was the least in this plant amongst all the public sector steel plants in the country, as originally planned. NINL had only 1352 executive and non-executive staff. Deployment of outsourced manpower through various agencies on contract basis was 1306. The contrast has to be seen in the context of overmanning in the public sector.

The Sum and Substance

At the end of the day, it is neither a story about the public sector nor about a steel project of MMTC. It is a story of the human spirit, human endeavour, entrepreneurship, grit and determination, garnering human cooperation; and faith in the bureaucracy, the politicians, and our system and in our own men and women; testing and transcending all limits of policies, procedures and personalities; and decision making in hazy and uncertain conditions and assuming responsibility for seeing it through its implementation, irrespective of the circumstances.

It is also a story of a team which was prepared to put its neck on the block for the sake of a mission in which it believed. Finally, it is not a story of certain specially gifted individuals who succeeded, but that of the common people, who believed in their mission and were prepared to work for it and assume responsibility, no matter what.

Most limits on human achievement are self-imposed. Battles are first fought in the head and heart before they are in the battle field. This is not to say that there are no insurmountable problems. There are; but more insurmountable problems are self-created than those created by the system or the situation.

That is why it is fair to believe that a lot can be achieved within the present system of the public sector. But, of course, much more can be achieved by reforming it and there is no justification for not doing so.

An analysis of what needs to be reformed and how to do so has been dealt in the next chapter.

6

Turnaround of the Public Sector

A LOT CAN BE ACHIEVED EVEN WITHIN THE CONSTRAINTS OF the present system, yet all public sector employees complain of many problems that prevent them from achieving their full potential, such as a lack of autonomy to take major decisions, political and bureaucratic interference, absence of freedom to incur adequate capital expenditure and invest in joint ventures and subsidiaries; as also to engage in mergers and acquisitions; crippling role of the investigation machinery and vigilance; multipoint audit by the internal auditors, CAG and Parliament; non-availability of freedom to fix their emoluments in line with the market; and lack of powers to take disciplinary action against their employees without review by the government; and above this, all the guidelines of the BPE that restrict freedom in important matters.

The PSEs do not have the power to recruit top management and create vacancies at senior levels. They are seriously concerned about falling under the definition of 'State', because of which they become as answerable as the government is to various organs of the state like the Parliament, investigative agencies, and the courts. This compromises their decision making and drags them in unnecessary and often frivolous litigation.

They have to be a role model for being an ideal and inclusive employer. The media also exposes them more than the private sector, simply because of their higher transparency and easier access to their confidential information. Unlike the private sector, they keep running a totally avoidable hurdle race, which wastes colossal amount of productive time.

The Solution So Far

Many remedies/reforms have been suggested in the past by committees and individuals like the LK Jha Committee (1981); Arjun Sengupta Committee (1984); Economic Advisory Council to the Prime Minister chaired by Sukhumoy Chakravarty (1987); N Vittal Committee Report on Rationalisation of the guidelines of the BPE; Rangarajan Committee Report (1993); etc. The other major milestones in this process were the policy pursued by the government of privatising the non-strategic enterprises from 1999–2000 to 2003–04; formation of the Disinvestment Commission and its subsequent burial; partial and lukewarm disinvestment of non-strategic PSEs except the Navratnas during the UPA 1 regime; and the latest decision of the UPA 2 to disinvest up to 10% shareholding in the listed companies and enlist the profit making companies on the stock exchanges for disinvestment; and creation of National Investment Fund (NIF) where the proceeds of disinvestment are vested and now permitting fresh disinvestment proceeds to be used for the social schemes of the government for the next three years, etc.

The Navratnas, Mini Ratnas, and Non-Ratnas

Some time ago, the government gave limited autonomy to a few Central Public Sector Enterprises (CPSEs) and called them Navratnas (nine jewels), Mini Ratnas–1 and Mini Ratnas–2. They have been delegated some powers on a graduated scale to incur capital expenditure, enter into strategic alliances and technology agreements, set up joint ventures, acquisitions and mergers, and approve tour programmes of their directors up to five days in an emergency. These powers, however, can be exercised subject to a number of conditions, including that of appointment of non-official independent directors by the government, which are sometimes difficult to comply with. Since the government took a long time in deciding the independent directors, many companies could not use these delegated powers for a long time. All the same, this is a definite step forward for these enterprises.

The number of such Navratna and Mini Ratna CPSEs was only nine and fifty, respectively (out of a total of 244, operational 217, as of 2006–07), according to Public Enterprises Survey of 2005–06.

The Non-Ratna companies, which form the majority, however have not been given such powers. Essentially, autonomy is the minimum condition for good performance for all the companies and not merely the Navratnas and, therefore, they too should be considered at par. Only those companies, which are financially dependent on the government, should seek prior approval.

The way some of the political executives choose independent directors to grant the powers to incur capital expenditure and use other delegated powers to the Navratna enterprises is also open to question.

Here is an example:

A young lady who used to be a student union leader till recently got nominated as an independent director in preference to a retired deputy governor of RBI, a chief secretary and a chairman and managing director of a leading PSE. But to be fair to this young lady, she was at least educated. This system of patronage has the potential of deteriorating even further.

Failure to Provide the Right Solution

The recommendations made by these committees would have substantially eased problems, had they been fully implemented. But this has not happened. The autonomy remains a distant dream. It appears that the political will to grant autonomy and reform the public sector is weak.

Shedding Majority Shareholding

These problems can be substantially solved if the shareholding of the government can be reduced to a minority, say below 50%. Then these organisations will cease to come under the definition of the 'State' under Article 12 of the Constitution and their decisions will not be subject to judicial review in terms of Article 14. They will also not be subject to review by the CAG, investigative agencies and Parliament. State functionaries will also not feel entitled to interfere. The PSEs will be able to recruit their own top management and others, fix emoluments in line with the market and take disciplinary action without any review by the government. This will make them truly board-managed and autonomous.

Four Dimensions of Turnaround

Here are some suggestions:

1. **Shed majority shareholding to grant autonomy**

However, granting autonomy alone is not a *sufficient condition* for improving effectiveness and efficiency but is the *minimal condition*. This is an enabler for the public sector to perform.

2. **Shed management control**

   The issue of who wields the management control is also crucial. It is possible for the government to reduce its shareholding below 50% and yet exercise management control as the majority shareholder, just as many private companies do. If it does not shed control, most problems, which need to be removed, will creep back through the back door. Hence management control should not be in the hands of the government.

3. **Empowerment for top-level recruitments**

   The boards of companies should have the power to recruit their top management and others.

4. **The human dimension**

   However, even if all the three issues are taken care of, it will only be in the direction of merely achieving technical efficiency. The solution must benefit people working in it and other stakeholders. *People are the purpose. This is the fourth dimension of the turnaround.*

SOLUTION

Privatisation

Privatisation is the key element. However, it is not really a remedy to improve the public sector, because after privatisation, it will be a private company trying to improve another company that was once a PSE. Such a privatised company is likely to lose the much needed public purpose and flavour.

Limitations of privatisation

Privatisation is not a panacea for improvement of its ills, as management of all private companies is not always benign.

Besides, there are many company, industry, technology and corporate governance issues which have to be individually tackled. Each company needs a different recipe at different stages of its growth and the context to solve specific problems and exploit opportunities. This can be done only by a competent professional management, irrespective of the ownership issue.

Privatisation does not automatically solve the problems of the employees of the PSEs. In many cases, it accentuates them. It only changes the ownership structure and achieves some technical efficiency. Many a times, it fails in the fourth dimension. If the private management is incompetent or malicious, it may fail to achieve even the technical efficiency and may also indulge in asset stripping.

Advantages of privatisation

However, privatisation has many advantages. It can usually perform on economic parameters which will increase the much desired rate of return on the capital employed and equity, and achieve other technical efficiencies.

Quality of Management

Whether they will actually turn the corner after privatisation depends on the quality, resources, intent and practices of good corporate governance. Solving problems, exploiting opportunities and driving growth, however, will depend on the competence of the new management. Privatisation is not the panacea to solve these management-related issues, but it offers a reasonably good solution despite limitations.

There are good and bad companies in both the sectors.

While the spotlight is on a few PSEs, which have not done well, no research has been carried to estimate how many private companies have fared badly, closed down, sacked their employees, not returned the loans to the public sector banks or declared bankruptcy, and indulged in financial irregularities. It is a misnomer that the public sector alone uses public money; the private companies borrow most of their investment money from public sector banks and financial institutions. One just has to look at the non-performing assets of the banks to know the enormity of misuse by some of the private companies. The number of such badly managed, failed or sick companies on life support administered by public money is, perhaps, much higher than that of the failed PSEs.

Some firms are managed atrociously and flout all norms of corporate governance and ethics. Remember Enron, WorldCom and Arthur Andersons? One has recently witnessed the shameful Satyam scandal and the alleged role played by the local partners of Price Waterhouse, all well-known names. The world keeps on sending similar reminders, such as the recent meltdown of the global financial markets caused primarily by private greed, which resulted in global recession from which the world has yet to recover. There has been widespread resentment in the USA and elsewhere where huge bailout packages have been provided to bail out some of them, once considered icons of the private sector.

There is a lack of wisdom in the blind acceptance of the privatisation recipe recommended by the IMF and the Washington Consensus. If one wants to understand the real motives and nexus of the IMF, one should read *Globalization and Its Discontents* by Joseph Stiglitz (Allen Lane, Penguin Press, 2002). Stiglitz was the winner of the Nobel Prize for Economics in 2001. He was the chief economist of the World Bank till 2000 and the chairman of President Bill Clinton's council of economic advisors.

Privatisation may be useful only if it takes place in favour of the companies that have good corporate governance, resources and the willingness to invest in improvements and the humaneness to treat public sector employees who join them. This requires suitable pre-qualification criteria.

On the other hand, while few CPSEs are making losses, including many private failed companies that had to be taken over by the government, the majority is making profits. The profitability has improved considerably after 1991, though not because of the reforms but in spite of them. The top 20 market cap companies in the Stock Exchanges include seven PSEs. The ratio of 13:7 in this pecking order between the two sectors on percentage basis is actually heavily loaded in favour of the public sector, when one considers that there are only 217 working CPSEs as against thousands of private companies in the country.

The two companies that created the maximum wealth by way of market cap during 2008 are NMDC and MMTC, both PSEs — according to the *Economic Times* dated April 3, 2008.

Hesitant Privatisation and Disinvestment Policy

Very few companies have so far been privatised in India. According to the public sector survey of 2005–06, the list of such companies includes BALCO, VSNL, CMC, Maruti, HZL, IPCL, HTL, IBP, PPL, MFIL, JCL, and ANIFDC, and a few properties of ITDC and HCI. The government has transferred management control to the private sector in these entities.

The government has also disinvested minor shareholding in many listed PSEs but continues to retain the management control. According to a 2006–07 survey, the number of CPSEs on the stock exchange was 44. According to the Economic Survey relating to 2006–07, the proceeds from disinvestment of all kinds from April 1991 to March 2006 amounted to only Rs. 49,241 crore. This is a small amount as compared with its potential.

Our privatisation policy has ranged from minor disinvestment during 1991–99 retaining the management control with the government to major strategic disinvestment during 1999–2004, where management control was vested in strategic investors. During the UPA 1 regime, the pendulum had swung back to keeping the management control in all profit-making enterprises with the government.

According to a UPA Government decision dated Nov 25, 2005, the emphasis was to list large profitable CPSEs on domestic stock exchanges and to selectively sell small portions of equity in listed profitable enterprises (other than the Navratnas), ensuring that the majority shareholding remained with the state.

In its second innings, without support of the Left, the record of privatisation has not been impressive so far. However, the Cabinet has taken the following important decisions regarding disinvestment on November 5, 2009:

- All listed profit-making public sector enterprises will have to off-load a minimum 10% equity stake. There are 10 such undertakings and the government hopes to raise from them more than Rs. 25,000 crore, out of which MMTC alone is expected to fetch more than Rs. 14,000 crore. Soon after the announcement, the price of one share of MMTC having a face value of Rs. 10 had shot up to Rs. 36,146 and its market cap had risen to a whopping Rs. 1,80,734 crore on November 6, 2009.

- The unlisted PSEs that meet the three criteria will have to opt for listing on the stock exchanges and could divest up to 10% of government's equity. The three such criteria are a positive net worth, a net profit for three consecutive years, and no accumulated losses. Such undertakings shall require the Cabinet's approval before disinvesting.

The disinvestment announced now is in sync with the earlier announcements and decisions, including the commitment to ensure that the state holding does not fall below 50%, except that they can now disinvest in the Navratna CPSEs too. However, now the scale of disinvestment will be much higher.

The money which will thus be raised will be invested in the capital expenditure of the social sector during the next three years (2009–12) and not be frozen in the NIF. This decision has ostensibly been taken because the finances of the government are under pressure due to ambitious spending on the social sector, falling tax receipts and additional funds required for pump-priming the economy in the wake of the recession. This raised the fiscal deficit to an unsustainable level of 6.8% of the GDP, excluding the deficit of the states. Raising funds through disinvestment will reduce the need to borrow from the market and avert further pressure on the already precarious fiscal deficit.

This has come on the heels of the government's decision to reduce its stake in the seven PSEs. The NHPC, OIL, NTPC, SJVNL, and NMDC initial public offers have already hit the bourses, while those of EIL and REC were on course. During 2009, 14 PSEs had already raised Rs. 14,469 crore

This is a welcome step. However, disinvestment is again being done to fund the fiscal deficit but not to reform the public sector. The government needs to change its mindset of looking at disinvestment only as a means of reducing deficit.

It should look at it as an instrument of raising productivity of capital deployed in the public sector institutions and getting them rid of their ills.

Minority disinvestment of the order announced is not likely to have any positive impact on the capital productivity of the CPSEs and may not even help much in reforming the public sector. Therefore, one needs to look at some other remedies. The major reason for the tardy progress of disinvestment and privatisation is the lack of national consensus, resulting in a weak political will.

Alternative Privatisation

It is not essential that companies are run either by the private sector or the public sector and management control is vested in the owners. In both, the units are actually run by professional employees. Therefore, it is worthwhile creating a new sector of professional employees themselves. Let it be called the **professional sector**.

Composition of New Boards of PSEs

To start with, the existing boards of the PSEs may continue for practical reasons. When the terms of the existing incumbents come to an end, the board should make, at the recommendations of the board's search committees, fresh appointments of chairmen and managing directors and full-time board directors from amongst the leading professional managers in the country. These boards should be autonomous and fully empowered to take all the decisions like in a private enterprise.

The Proposal is in Three Parts

Alternative privatisation can be done first, in favour of the serving employees of the public sector; second, in favour of the surplus staff; and third, in favour of the private professionals, scientists, etc.

(A) Privatisation in favour of serving employees

Simply put, the proposed professional sector can be created by disinvesting about 74% shareholding of the government in the PSEs to the public at large/retail investors, the autonomous financial institutions of the government, and the balance 26% to the employees. The management control shall vest in the board of directors consisting of professional managers.

(B) Promoting new private companies to deploy the surplus staff

A small part of the disinvestment proceeds should be used to prepare many detailed project reports (DPRs) for new projects, which can absorb the surplus staff. Such small and medium enterprises (SMEs) shall be ex-employee-managed autonomous private units.

(C) Promoting new companies to deploy private professionals

Private employees and professionals, scientists and the academia could also be involved in these SMEs in a similar manner to supplement the competencies of the public sector surplus staff. They can even be invited and encouraged to form their own SMEs. The DPRs for such SMEs can be commissioned even on the behest of scientists and patent holders to encourage entrepreneurship based on applied research and innovations.

These proposals will help in promoting a new private professional sector in the country and the state should facilitate it.

The Scheme

The proposal to disinvest 74% to the public and 26% to the employees is oversimplified because first, our financial markets are not yet deep and broad enough to absorb the 74% divestment at one go. Second, our public sector employees cannot afford to buy 26% shareholding of their companies straightaway.

This is where the state can hold the hands of the employees, private professionals and the public retail investors, by stretching this process of disinvestment over a longer period, by bringing in intermediate institutional arrangements. Credit should also be extended by the banks, financial institutions and PSEs to their employees for buying the shares. Both the private and public sector companies have come up because of the heavy funding by the state institutions in the past.

Pending a national consensus on privatisation, the government should disinvest 74% shares to the retail investors. Whatever shares cannot be bought by the retail investors immediately may be sold to them, in stages, over time. In the meantime, the unsold block of shares may be sold to the government financial institutions. It may involve strengthening the capital base and the leveraging power of these financial institutions. In due course, the financial institutions should try to offload these balance shares gradually to the retail investors and the employees.

The current political opposition is not to disinvestment per se but disinvestment in favour of private business magnates and the companies managed by them. The public is wary of selling to them the family silver belonging to the tax payer. However, nobody is likely to object to divestment in favour of the retail investors.

Out of the balance 26% shareholding, the government may sell about 5% to the employees initially and another 2% may be granted free as sweat equity. The ownership of 7% will create a sense of partnership amongst the employees.

Since the employees of the public sector will not be able to afford to buy all the 26% shareholding meant for them at one go, an intermediate mechanism is required, in addition to the facility of granting loans by banks, etc. to buy shares.

The Special Purpose Vehicle: An Intermediate Institutional Mechanism

Set up an autonomous special purpose vehicle (SPV) as the medium of extending state support to all the actors involved in the alternative privatisation proposal at (A), (B), and (C).

The proceeds of 74% disinvestment in favour of retail investors/financial institutions, balance 19% (after giving 7% out of 26% to the employees) shareholding out of the employees' quota, and the unsold shareholding to the retail investors, employees and the financial institutions, if any, may be vested in this SPV. Thus, huge funds of disinvestment and unsold shareholding of the government would be vested in this SPV.

Composition of its Board of Directors

The SPV shall have its own autonomous board of directors, and should comprise senior public sector serving or retired chief executives/directors, directors of government financial institutions/banks, senior members of the academia from the select management institutes/IITs, and other private and public business professionals of national repute. The board should be headed by a retired or serving senior public sector chairman and managing director, as its full-time CEO. This board should have full-time directors. Independent directors to be nominated on this board should be former chairmen and managing directors of CPSEs, government financial institutions and public sector banks. This SPV should be an autonomous body, like the Election Commission of India or the Reserve Bank of India.

Professional Nominees of the SPV to Represent the Government

In addition to what has been stated in the previous section, the government should be represented on the boards of the PSEs by one or two professional nominees of the board of the SPV as independent directors or they could be directors of the SPV. This will ensure autonomy of the boards of the PSEs.

The board of the concerned PSE should also invite one or two independent directors of national repute from the same professional community in addition to the independent directors nominated by the SPV. This will have a balancing effect on the power of the SPV. The number of full-time and independent directors could be equal. The chairman of the board should have the casting vote in case of equal voting. The board should be compact and not unwieldy for effective decision making.

Shareholding of the employees (7%) and the remaining shareholding of the government in the employees' quota (19%) out of 26% should form one solid block of shares for voting to enable the employees to exercise effective control over board resolutions. In the case of some of the PSEs, it may be necessary to keep this block between 26% and 40% to prevent a hostile takeover. The SPV too should back this arrangement through their nominee directors for keeping the management control in the hands of the employees, even though they do not have a majority control at this juncture.

Over time, this SPV may try to shed the balance unsold shareholding in favour of the employees and the retail investors when they can afford to buy these shares.

If the government spreads disinvestment over longer time, it is likely to make much more money, and financial markets are not yet deep and broad enough to withstand simultaneous disinvestment of all the PSEs. The pace of disinvestment will have to be calibrated carefully. If the facility to extend the loans to the employees and the retail investors is created to buy shares, disinvestment to them shall pick up.

The proposal of *alternative privatisation* is calculated to create a huge private professional sector consisting of employees of the public sector, private professionals, scientists, patent holders of innovations, and the academia, with active promotional assistance from the proposed SPV, banks, etc.

Do a Pilot First

It is prudent to initially do a pilot in a non-strategic profitable PSE. This can be later expanded to all enterprises other than the critically sick and strategic.

Critically Sick and Strategic PSEs

The critically sick need to be closed down and their employees rehabilitated through the SPV. The critically strategic to national security may have to be retained in the public or state sector for some time. Possibility of a public–private partnership could be investigated in such units too, wherever feasible.

Win-Win Situation for all Stakeholders

Alternative privatisation, as suggested, would be reckoned a win-win situation by all concerned and it is likely to retain the public sector flavour, imbued with the much-needed public interest.

Employees Would Be Happy to Retain Jobs and Gain Autonomy and Wealth

After the government's shareholding falls below 50%, these PSEs shall cease to be 'State' under Article 12 of the Indian Constitution and their decisions will not be subject to judicial review in terms of Article 14. They will go out of the jurisdiction of the investigative agencies, parliamentary committees, vigilance and CAG. Their autonomous boards can then be authorised to make all those decisions which the private boards take. *This shall make them truly board-managed companies and please the employees.*

The public would be happy because millions of new retail shareholders would share the wealth created out of disinvestment of 74% holding of the government.

FORGING A POLITICAL CONSENSUS

The Left and other political parties, which are against disinvestment to the private business companies, will be happy that the business barons do not get away with the family silver, and the public at large is the gainer.

'*Aam Aadmi*', or the common man, will gain, which is claimed to be the political constituency of every political party. *Because of the political consensus on the common man and retention of public sector jobs, disinvestment will be allowed to be started by various political parties and the trade unions.*

This will enable the government to raise money through disinvestment which can be used to create a safety net for the workers and improve the health of the weaker public undertakings.

The Scheme Shall Immensely Please the Trade Unions

The funds created out of the disinvestment in the alternative model of privatisation in favour of professionals can be invested in funding the future growth of the public sector undertakings, helping the weaker PSEs, rehabilitation of workers, and promoting entrepreneurship amongst the professionals of the public and the private sectors, scientists, researchers and the academicians, and building infrastructure, education, and health.

After this proposal is adopted, the government can utilise the entire money lying in the NIF on their schemes of social development and infrastructure, as the SPV shall have enough funds of its own to finance the purposes listed. NIF can also be used for shoring up the capital base of the financial institutions and banks to enable them to purchase unsold shares to the retail investors and employees.

Outstripping Many a Reliance

Disinvestment on a large scale will create millions of retail investors that will outstrip many a Reliance, and broaden and deepen our financial markets. This will unleash further savings, investments, capital formation, economic development, and employment — that alone can reduce poverty.

Truly board-managed autonomous PSEs will ensure a much higher rate of return and productivity on huge investment of more than Rs. 4,21,089 crore made by the nation in the CPSEs. This will improve the global competitiveness of India.

Since the private professionals, scientists, and academicians can also join this sector, it will immensely help private professionals and make India a more innovative and globally competitive society. If this proposal is debated widely, there is a good possibility of finding consensus. Debate will bring in other expert inputs, which can hone this proposal further.

The Biggest Asset of India: The Professionals

One of the biggest assets of our nation are the professionals, who are likely to be the largest in the world. It is time to think beyond family owned businesses, traditional business magnates, and public sector, and create a new entrepreneurial class with some help from the state as suggested herein, by giving them ownership and higher incentives. Imagine the entrepreneurship it will unleash. As the entrepreneurship deepens and broadens, it will change the business landscape and spread the seeds of entrepreneurship, employment, and income throughout the country. It will lead to many other positive societal changes. The professionals-turned-entrepreneurs will boost the global comparative advantage.

Population Dividend

According to the Economic Survey of 2006–07, the well-known demographic dividend of India will manifest in the proportion of population in the working age group of 15–64 years increasing steadily from 62.5% in 2006 to 68.4% in 2026. The working age population in age group 15–59 by 2016–17 is going to be about 820 million, according to the Eleventh Five-Year-Plan document. India is going to overtake China in population by 2030.

India already has the youngest population in the world. Most of the developed western world and Japan are ageing. It is expected that the ageing economy phenomenon will globally create a skilled manpower shortage of about 56.5 million by 2020 and if we can get our skill development act right as envisaged in the Eleventh Five-Year Plan, there would be a skilled manpower surplus of about 47 million, which can fill this void. These demographic trends have already set in and demographics are the only certain thing about the future.

Therefore, India has a window of opportunity of about 25 years to harness the 'population dividend', provided it can educate and train people and look after the health of the nation. If we fail to do so, the so-called 'population dividend' will become a millstone around our neck.

The Third Sector of Professionals

The proposed *alternative privatisation* will indeed be a people-oriented solution. *Privatisation,* as popularly understood, and *alternative privatisation* are not mutually exclusive solutions and they can supplement each other. Both can be tried simultaneously, keeping the pros and cons in mind.

Ways to Work through the System

Till there is a consensus on privatisation or the alternative privatisation suggested for creating a new professional sector of entrepreneurs, there is no other option for public sector officers but to be strong, firm, tactful, and resist all interference. It is possible to do so.

The financially independent Non-Ratna companies should try to get similar powers of capital expenditure and investments as granted to the Navratna and Mini Ratna companies.

Bureaucracy, which has the art of persuading the political class, is the best bet for the public sector to draw support from. Many ministers are also amenable, if the case is explained to them in terms of the political gain.

It is generally seen that the public sector is reluctant to use even whatever power is delegated to it, because employees are unnecessarily worried about minding their backs for fear of investigations. They must use their powers, and sometimes even go beyond them, by taking the government into confidence. Delegations and powers have meaning only if they are exercised.

It is suggested that till the reforms of the public sector are carried out, let the PSEs continue reporting to the administrative ministries, sign MOUs with them and be accountable for performance. However, the government directors, who are appointed on the boards of the PSEs, should be nominated from a ministry/department other than the administrative ministry.

This will ensure better objectivity and independence than the present practice of nominating the directors from the administrative ministry, some of whom have the tendency to lose objectivity because of the intense day-to-day relationship with the PSEs and a tendency to control them.

This practice shall ensure a modicum of objectivity and neutrality. The government could nominate equivalent ranked officers from the specialists' organisations too on their boards. Preferably, there should be only one or maximum two such directors on the PSE boards.

The chairman should send to the government a confidential report of such directors on their contribution and performance, which should be incorporated in the annual confidential reports written by their reporting officers.

The government directors should be held equally responsible and accountable for the overall performance of the PSEs like the other directors. They should not be mere auditors or monitors but should contribute to building the present and the future of these companies. The work load of the senior officers of the government in the ministries is very heavy and the responsibilities are onerous, because of which they do not get time to do justice to the board positions of many companies. Therefore, they should not be burdened with the directorship of more than 2/3 PSEs. However, they should be paid the fee given to independent directors for attending board meetings.

Abandon the Old and the Unsustainable

The government should abandon the terminally sick PSEs or very sick units or those which cannot be quickly turned around. Societies which do not abandon in time pay a very heavy price for lethargy. India has not learnt its lessons yet. The suggested SPV should be able to take care of the rehabilitation concerns of the surplus employees. There is no point in throwing good money after bad money once the surplus employees are rehabilitated.

An Entrepreneurial Approach to Rehabilitation

There is naturally a resistance amongst the employees who have to be laid off. So far, the government has looked at the solution in terms of voluntary retirement compensation only. Here is a new approach which can be experimented with.

The PSEs should prepare lists of the surplus employees and send them to the SPV.

Creation of Many New Private SMEs

The rehabilitation division of the proposed SPV should get consultants to *prepare project reports* for a number of new projects/ SMEs which can be set up where the surplus employees can be accommodated.

Seed Money and Working Capital

The seed money for such projects may be provided by this autonomous SPV as equity and initial working capital, including the salaries for say two to four years, and bank guarantees.

After two to four years, these companies should be on their own as independent businesses and all funding from the SPV should stop. These SMEs shall have to return to the SPV the money lent by it along with the interest.

Disinvestment of Equity Held by the SPV

Much of the initial equity of the new companies will be taken up by this autonomous SPV. Its disinvestment in such entrepreneurial units, in favour of the employees and the retail investors after about three to four years, should follow a similar route for the professional sector of serving PSE employees.

Conceptually, look at all the surplus employees and those seeking voluntary retirement as one big pool. This will comprise of officers, white-collared and blue-collared workers coming from different companies and having diverse competencies. Once the project reports for the new projects are ready based on which decisions are made for setting up certain projects keeping in mind the competencies of this pool, separate independent companies may be formed. Suitable officers, workers and staff may be allocated, after ascertaining the preferences.

Whatever compensation is to be paid as voluntary retirement benefits may be given in the shape of shares. The employees may also be granted some free shares towards sweat equity. Those who do not want to participate in this scheme may be paid voluntary retirement benefits in cash by this SPV.

Composition of the Board

Initially, the full-time board directors should be selected from the officers in this pool through a system of interviews to be conducted by a selection committee appointed by the board of the proposed SPV. Part-time directors may be appointed from the serving or retired or retiring officers of the public sector, financial institutions, banks, private companies, and management academicians. In addition, the new company could invite two leading similar professionals to serve as independent directors on their boards.

The ex-employee entrepreneurs should be encouraged to buy controlling shares of this company in due course. The balance shares can be held in the interim period by the SPV and the financial institutions.

Such companies should be private as government will not have any direct shareholding in them. The SPV will substitute the government in this case and gradually disinvest the shares to the employees, the public, financial institutions, and the banks, etc. The financial institutions may also follow suit for shedding shares to the employees and retail investors over a period of time.

This SPV is not an institution to promote new public sector units. It is rather an institution to provide seed capital and promote new entrepreneurs in the private sector. This will provide a great fillip to the expansion of the SMEs.

The boards should be autonomous on the lines suggested for the new professional sector companies of serving employees. They should take all future decisions on further investments, the scope of their activities, hiring and firing including the future board members and the chairman and managing director, and the emoluments of people, etc. They should all be board-managed companies. If such companies find that they need a chief executive/full-time director or any other specialists from the market, they should be free to do so on emoluments that are in line with the market and their own structure of emoluments.

Management Control

Management control should vest with their boards even if the employees do not have majority shareholding. However, the promoter SPV should exercise the required control to safeguard their investment through their independent nominee directors on their boards.

It should be possible to float many private companies that will effectively deploy surplus public sector employees and also create fresh employment. Thus, a new entrepreneurial sector would come up. The employees who are considered a problem today will turn into assets and opportunities.

The surplus employees would welcome it as it will give them ownership and allow them to work with the old community of colleagues. Such units are likely to retain some public sector flavour and public purpose.

Such new entrepreneurial units will have to be self-sufficient financially after three to four years, depending on the nature of industry. After this, they should be on their own, return their loans with interest to the SPV, and prosper or perish like any other private company.

Today, after an employee seeks voluntary retirement, he/she finds it difficult to set up their own enterprise with the paltry benefits they get.

Debate on these Concepts Shall Enrich and Refine them

These are broad brush concepts and can undergo a change as they are debated. For instance, whether there should be one large SPV or more than one can be debated. It is possible to have one SPV for representing interests of the government on the boards of PSEs of the serving employees, another one for rehabilitation of the surplus staff and creating new entrepreneurial entities in the private sector, and still another for infrastructure or education or health. A lot of fresh thinking will have to be done to hone practical proposals out of these broad suggestions.

Role of State Governments

The methodology suggested for the CPSEs can be adopted by state governments too for their public sector undertakings, with minor modifications to suit their specific needs. The suggested SPV could possibly contribute partly to the fund of similar state SPVs.

However, the state governments shall have to close more sick units than the centre as sickness is more rampant in the states.

Summing Up

The public sector is hedged in by constraints, which prevent it from achieving optimum productivity and the rate of return on heavy investments. It needs autonomy to tackle such constraints and perform effectively.

The efforts made so far, like partial privatisation, without the government losing control on the management, and removal of some guidelines of the BPE, etc. to reform the public sector and remove their constraints, have failed to ease the problems. Progress of these reforms has been tardy, partly because of a failure to forge a political consensus on privatisation and disinvestment.

Therefore, *alternative privatisation* in favour of the serving PSE employees, surplus staff, private professionals, scientists, patent holders, management professionals, and academia has been proposed. This scheme and the SPV suggested to facilitate it are calculated to create a new professional sector which will fill the global shortage of skilled people, through availability of young professionals that India alone can provide in large numbers. This will enable exploitation of the *population dividend* during the next twenty-five years or so.

This will generate new employment that will help in reducing poverty and making the economic progress more inclusive and widely dispersed. State help for creating the institutional framework of the suggested SPV and spreading the disinvestment process over a longer period to make it affordable, and the facility to get loans to buy shares will go a long way in facilitating it.

Rehabilitation of surplus staff, as suggested in the entrepreneurial solution, is a much better way than giving them one-time voluntary retirement benefits. *Alternative privatisation* is likely to meet all the four dimensions of public sector turnaround contained herein and remove its proverbial problems. Because of this, there is a possibility of evolving a political consensus on *alternative privatisation*.

Both the solutions of *privatisation*, as normally understood, and *alternative privatisation* suggested here supplement each other and can be tried simultaneously, depending upon the merits and demerits of each case, to remove the constraints. It has been suggested that the states can adopt a similar scheme to reform their public sector.

7

NEGOTIATIONS IN JAPAN

MANY INDIAN COMPANIES AND EXECUTIVES HAVE TO negotiate with their Japanese counterparts for exports, imports, foreign collaboration, and joint venture agreements. Some of them find it difficult to break the ice as Japan is relatively an opaque and difficult market.

One of the highest exports from India to Japan was that of iron ore. The value of the five-year contract MMTC negotiated (divided into five annual contracts), at today's prices would be above Rs. 7000 crore (Rs. 3500 crore then). This brought the company in close contact with the seven major Japanese steel mills (JSMs) and major Japanese trading companies (JTCs), which coordinated on their behalf.

Consortium of the Japanese Steel Mills

The JSMs, to which MMTC supplied iron ore regularly, included Nippon Steel, Sumitomo Metal, Kobe Steel, Kawasaki Steel, NKK, Nisshin Steel, and Nakayama Steel, all of which bought in a consortium. These steel mills appointed JTCs as chief coordinators in India to liaise with the suppliers, government and others. Such JTCs included Okura, Nissho Iwai, Mitsui, Mitsubishi, Marubeni, Itochu, Nomura, Kanematsu, and some others. Okura and company was the chief coordinator for MMTC at that time.

I had an opportunity to work in Marubeni Corporation, a major Japanese company, as an advisor, and looked into its working, ethos, and culture, and was also a member of the Indo-Japanese Standing Committee.

Role of the Japanese Trading Companies in Negotiations

The representatives of Okura used to meet MMTC officers for ironing out difficulties in shipments of iron ore, keeping it informed about what the JSMs were contemplating, and trying to gauge reaction to their thinking and our approach to the forthcoming annual negotiations.

They were assessing our situation constantly and giving feedback to their head offices. Their knowledge about the Indian ports, shipment difficulties, quality problems, problems of wagons in India, and difficulties of JSMs with the Indian iron ore was impressive. They were in regular touch with the senior officials in our Ministries of Commerce, Mines and Steel to assess how much high-grade Bailadila ore would be permitted to be exported and changes likely in the state policy.

They would sensitise MMTC about the concerns of JSMs and vice versa. They knew the situation of the global steel industry, total production of steel expected, and likely consumption of iron ore in the wake of new demand and supply situation. They were abreast with the latest developments in negotiations in Europe, Brazil, Australia, Russia, etc.

This is a beautiful role model for a liaison agent of any company. But what is of concern here is the immense preparation in collecting the quantity and quality of information at the pre-negotiation stage by the Japanese. Many Indian companies do not take the pains to go that far in doing so, thus yielding an advantage to their counterparts. Thorough preparation is a very important stage of negotiations, which negotiators can ignore at their own risk. Japan was an excellent role model.

Home Work at Pre-Negotiation and Preparation Stages

The Japanese do their homework meticulously to evolve, develop and drive a helpful agenda, know who will lead the Indian delegation and his/her background and also that of the other members of the delegation. They even resented when a bureaucrat led the negotiations though he was officiating as the chairman of MMTC, as they feared that he might adopt a more rigid approach than a commercial person. This is the kind of preparation done by Japan even at the pre-negotiation stage. MMTC too adopted the same strategy.

It matters who is at the table on the other side. It can be very frustrating if your actual decision makers are at the negotiating table but the counterparts keep themselves in the background, from whom approvals have to be sought before any decision. Negotiations between people having unequal authority in their respective organisations can prove frustrating. That is why maintaining a protocol is important, as is generally the case in the negotiations between two governments.

Fulcrum of Negotiations

Japan attaches a high premium on the supply of high-grade Bailadila iron ore lumps/fines from India, produced by NMDC and marketed by MMTC to the JSMs. Therefore, the Japanese try to maximise the purchase of this ore. India/MMTC tries to sell the maximum quantity of Indian low-grade iron ore from the eastern coast, as it supports the employment of poor people, and tries to restrict the supply of high-grade ore from Bailadila since it is required for domestic consumption. Achieving the balance becomes the fulcrum of negotiations.

MMTC was fully aware that if India did not supply enough of high-grade Bailadila lumps, the Japanese would cover their requirements from Brazil. They would then also not pick up our low-grade iron ore from eastern India and instead buy it from Australia; MMTC would be forced to keep excessive inventory of low-grade ores. This was Japan's best alternative to the negotiated agreement (BATNA), if the negotiations failed.

India's BATNA or fall back was to sell the high-grade Bailadila ores in the domestic market, which was clamouring to save high-grade *lumps* for their use. But it had relatively low domestic demand for Bailadila high-grade *fines,* considering the high inventory with NMDC and even lower demand for the low-grade ores of eastern India; this weakened our BATNA, if the negotiations failed, since low-grade eastern ores were our Achilles' heel.

Every skilful negotiator should try to strengthen his BATNA and reduce that of the other party.

Bottle of Brandy and the Bitter Medicine

A few months before the negotiations, it was observed that Japan actually nominated more vessels for Bailadila than for low-grade ores on a proportionate basis. This had resulted in comparatively lower lifting of the low-grade ores from India, though a higher quantity had been ordered. However, the entire quota of Bailadila high-grade lumps had been lifted well before the end of the year. It, perhaps, conveniently forgot to nominate a few vessels for low-grade ores. The matter needed to be sorted out with the Japanese.

This sensitive issue was raised on the second day of the negotiations with the leader of the Japanese delegation in a full meeting. The meeting started with the narration of a story about a drunkard who fell seriously sick. The doctor prescribed six doses of medicine and one spoon of brandy every day. When the doctor came to check the patient after a week, he discovered that the bottle of brandy was already finished and only one dose of medicine had been consumed.

It was politely brought to the delegation's notice that the JSMs were like that patient who promptly finished the bottle of brandy but found excuses for not consuming the medicine. It was duly amplified that their bottle of brandy was high-grade Bailadila lumps and their medicine was low-grade ore from the eastern coast of India. It must be pointed out that the joke was taken in the right spirit and resulted in sombre atmosphere of the negotiations becoming very light and friendly. A five-year contract was signed on satisfactory terms, and a good and fair balance achieved between what was wanted by the JSMs and what India needed.

Japan Set the Global Benchmark of Price

These negotiations were held by a delegation of seven major JSMs, led by the general manager of the Nippon Steel Mills, who was assisted by a co-leader from the Sumitomo Metals and 30–40 officers from the JSMs and JTCs. At that time, this consortium for buying iron ore was not only the biggest buyer of the world, but all the other major global buyers used the prices settled by it as the best global benchmark to settle their own prices. The Japanese were considered the smartest buyers of the world. China's demand for iron ore was not that high till then.

Since, the JSMs bought in a consortium, they reduced BATNA, though India also responded by forming a consortium of suppliers. But the biggest buyers of the world had an upper hand.

Now, of course, India's biggest export of iron ore is to China.

Preparations before Negotiations with the Japanese

Loose remarks and wrong claims are not tolerated. This brings down credibility irretrievably. The preparation for negotiations with the Japanese must be very thorough. The negotiators must be aware of the full history of the past dealings, rectification of any complaints forwarded, supply and demand gap of product and industry and global and national factors which could affect the prices and availability of a product, etc.

Dinner Diplomacy

Large suppliers are normally treated with courtesy and respect. Their trading companies invite delegations to dinners. A cautious approach is a must at such dinners, as the representatives of these JTCs are looking for constantly gauging and taking note of everything said that gives an inkling of the stance likely to be adopted in the formal negotiations. It is best to drink moderately.

Should One Request for Transport

It is preferable not to request the Japanese prospects to provide transport when on a visit to Japan, unless it is offered.

The Japanese are careful about using their car facility. In many trading companies, car pools are spun into separate cost centres or small companies to keep control on car use. The Narita Airport is also very far from the Tokyo city and it is unreasonable to expect them to arrange any concierge.

Gifts

It is customary to take some gifts for the customers. Even when the gifts are sent to the homes or offices, the Japanese acknowledge them during open meetings. The same practice should be followed when gifts are brought to India, notwithstanding the *sarkari Farash Khana culture*, where government (*sarkari*) officials have to deposit gifts beyond a small value in a *Farash Khana* (warehouse). Indian tea, handicrafts, silk, artefacts, and deluxe Scotch whisky, etc. are appreciated as gifts.

Schedule Meetings Well in Advance

Do not try to show familiarity with the Japanese or suddenly invite them for a meal. Normally, it is best to fix all the appointments and social engagements including dinners well before leaving India. No Japanese normally meets without prior appointment. Disruption in schedule is not taken to kindly.

People are Similar Everywhere

Though people of different countries look so different on the surface, they are the same everywhere. If there are genuine concerns for interests of others, it is reciprocated. If one tries to act smart, you can be beaten at the game. There could be some exceptions, which will have to be dealt with more firmly.

Business is built on relations; and relations are based on human nature, which is the same everywhere. It transcends all barriers of language and culture. The body language tells a foreign prospect if someone is trustworthy. Nothing pays more than sincerity and integrity, coupled with competence and effective execution of contracts and promises.

Punctuality

It is a universal rule to be punctual for appointments. Occupy the allotted seat in a conference room 5–10 minutes before the scheduled time.

In discussions, it is better to promise less and deliver more rather than the other way round. It is also a universal rule that in all dealings with human beings, unselfishness pays more than selfishness and foreigners are no exception to this rule. Take care of the customer and he/she reciprocates, irrespective of the cultural differences. Of course, both the sides have to watch their respective turfs.

Negotiations

Keep in mind the basics:

1. Objective in the context of your ground realities;
2. Perception of objective of the opposite party in the context of ground realities;
3. Extent of a possible compromise by both parties in view of respective objectives beyond which they will be ready to walk out. Be prepared with the give and take possibilities;
4. What can be the acceptable compromise whereby both the parties gain and proclaim victory to their respective constituencies? Out-of-box thinking can help in developing such alternatives to create value;
5. Offer a face-saving device to the opposite party keeping in mind the psyche of the constituency it has to satisfy;

6. Preparation for the negotiations should start by being the devil's advocate and working out all the arguments the opposite party can bring up to make a formidable case;
7. During negotiations, start by laying on the table full claims with justifications and request for the ideal outcome you would like to achieve. No compromise should be offered at this stage. The opposite party is likely to do the same;
8. Compromises may have to be considered as negotiations progress. Ultimately, most agreements involve compromises, but if you offer a compromise right in the beginning, you miss the chance of achieving the ideal outcome. Compromise options must be closer to the objective or mission, and not away from it;
9. Listen carefully and watch the body language of the opposite party. Try to address its concerns. Empathy is important;
10. Translate for the other party the apparent advantages being ceded in the negotiations into its own benefits. It is difficult but not impossible. For instance, if the opposite party agrees to concede higher price for the product, tell it how the upgraded quality and service being provided in return shall benefit it;
11. Respect and treat the other party at an equal level.

Organisational Negotiation Competency

When a large number of individuals are proficient in negotiations, the organisation itself becomes proficient in this art. But there is one problem. Good negotiators have to leave due to retirement, change of job, or assignment. The knowledge of negotiations and skills required to conduct them gets destroyed or transferred in the process and the organisations are deprived of those skills. Therefore, there has to be a method to store the experiences and skills of the individuals and groups in a knowledge bank, which can be easily retrieved by the new negotiators and made applicable in similar situations to avoid inventing the wheel, time and again. Relations and contacts must also be transferred to the successors, for which the companies should introduce a suitable mechanism.

Even negotiation has to be viewed as a process and not an individual event. The process approach enables the process to become better at every stage: pre-negotiation, preparation, actual negotiation, concluding deals, and their acceptance by stakeholders of the negotiating parties, learning from negotiations and storing in a knowledge bank for easy retrieval.

The steps mentioned should improve the organisational negotiation competency.

Merger and Acquisition

These principles are equally useful while negotiating merger and acquisition (M&A) deals.

Of course, there are many things to remember, when it comes to negotiations for M&A, like how to screen potential candidates for M&A; proceed with pre-negotiations; reach initial agreement; conduct Due Diligence; set final terms; negotiate a good price; negotiate alternative M&A deal to have a choice; how much to pay in stocks and how much in cash; when to get up from the table and stop negotiations; how to manage the deal; how to bring about integration between two companies and what kind of a person should become the integration manager; how to merge cultures of the two companies and how to manage ego and interests of major players of both sides; how to harvest the intended economic benefits of mergers and acquisitions; and finally, how to sell the deal to the stakeholders of both the companies.

A Win-Win Situation for Both the Parties

A negotiation is an opportunity to forge a new relationship and partnership and not merely a good agreement. Both parties must win for the agreement to be durable. Such deals are known as *integrative negotiation deals.* They are particularly important where long-term relations between parties matter. In fact, most deals should be negotiated in this manner.

However, in transient relationships, where people are not likely to cross each other's path again, they try to extract the maximum value at the expense of the other party and in some such cases this behaviour can be justified or, at least, condoned. Such one-way deals are known as *distributive negotiation deals*.

However, when negotiators try to treat an integrative deal like a distributive deal and extract value from the other party in a selfish fashion, they miss a great opportunity of out-of-box thinking to create new value for the larger good of both the parties and building a durable relationship that would have yielded to them in the future many more such deals and perennial profit.

Negotiations between two parties are easier to handle. However, multi-party negotiations are complex and difficult. A case in point is the iron ore deal between MMTC and the JSMs. The major players were the seven large steel mills of Japan on the one hand, and a group of MMTC, NMDC, Kudremukh Iron Ore Company Limited (KIOCL), a large number of iron ore miners of India, Ministry of Steel, Ministry of Commerce and other policy making organs of the government, on the other.

MMTC had to manage lot of shadow boxing to finally take an agreed stand on the basket of high-grade and low-grade lumps and fines each player could spare. Gruelling internal negotiations took place throughout the year amongst all these groups.

Wage Settlement Negotiations between NALCO and its Trade Unions

Here is an example of a win-win/integrative negotiation based on creating value on shared interests. A board committee of NALCO, the largest alumina and aluminium producer, which included a senior joint secretary and a former chairman of MMTC, was able to revise a wage agreement with the unions that had threatened a major strike, by trading extra benefits to the staff to achieve the best global benchmarks of performance for productivity and better discipline. NALCO, the unions and the government gained, and it did not cost the unions anything, except better discipline.

The negotiation focussed on increasing welfare of every stake holder and increasing the size of the cake to be shared. Therefore, the negotiation succeeded even in a highly embarrassing situation. This may perhaps be the only wage settlement agreement in the public sector where the unions agreed to achieve the best global benchmarks of performance. In a way, it also set the agenda for the management too, which had failed thus far to achieve these benchmarks.

The unions went out of the way to cooperate to improve work practices, work culture, and discipline. The production and productivity of NALCO recorded impressive increase in line with best global benchmarks. This is exemplary because such execution has not been usually witnessed to achieve best global benchmarks in many PSEs, thanks to the constant monitoring by their board.

This case study provides an excellent example of how a distributive negotiation, where one party wanted to claim the maximum value for itself, was converted into a successful integrative negotiation.

Creating value, by understanding the whole situation of the other party and creating synergy between the negotiating parties, as done in the case of NALCO, is one of the most important individual and organisational negotiation capabilities. This example can be emulated by other managements to not only achieve the best global benchmarks but to exceed them.

PEC and the Cotton Corporation of India

In negotiations, our key aim should be to build on shared interests to forge win-win agreements. However, differences between parties can also be a source of creating value.

PEC was to export cotton to Vietnam for the first time in 1991-92.The supplier was the Cotton Corporation of India. The chairman of Cotton Corporation did not want to take the risk of exporting through certain ports in Vietnam. However, at PEC, there was a different risk appetite and perception of Vietnamese ports and it offered to undertake this risk, provided it was paid an additional commission — which was accepted. By exploiting the difference in risk appetite and perceptions of risk, there is always a scope to negotiate a win-win agreement quickly.

PEC won the contract and cotton worth Rs. 17 crore was duly supplied at the desired ports. Both the companies gained in the deal. PEC traded its different risk appetite and risk perception to create a higher value for both.

8

Buying Processes of Japan, China, and India

THE JAPANESE ARE AMONGST THE SMARTEST BUYERS of the world. Take iron ore for instance. Japan was the largest importer of iron ore of the world till the 1990s. Now China has emerged the largest buyer. Each of the seven major JSMs was large enough a buyer to command favourable prices; yet none of these companies bought on its own. They formed a consortium comprising of some of the biggest manufacturers of the world and this gave them the muscle to lord over the miners and suppliers.

Buying is a Process

They did not float any tenders. They did not buy in one fell swoop. They did not invite offers to shortlist prequalified suppliers. They followed a unique buying process. Purchasing was not a mere transaction, it was instead a process — an year-long process.

The raw material department conducted a year-long research on factors that affected the price directly and indirectly like health of the steel industry throughout the world; health of economies; demand and supply of iron ore in each country and the world; demand and supply of pig iron and steel which was the user of iron ore and the state of raw materials required by them; the state of health of industries consuming steel; and shifting patterns of production between the blast furnace and arc furnace steel plants that affected the demand, as the latter do not consume iron ore, etc.

They also researched on subjects like shipping and transport conditions in the supplier countries; quality standards maintained and efforts made to adhere to standards set by them; health of the mines; export policy of the governments; conditions prevailing in their own steel mills and total real cost of each ore when finally used in the JSMs; and the imbalance between demand and supply during the year, etc.

Each steel mill had one or two trading companies (JTCs) that acted as their representatives. The liaison offices of the JTCs in India, Brazil, and Australia, kept in constant touch with the suppliers, ports, railways, miners, and their respective governments to reflect the views of the JSMs and vice versa.

Commercial Diplomacy or Commercial Judo

The Japanese are adept at the game of judo, the objective being to make the opponent submit using minimum force. Peter F. Drucker, the father of modern management, has termed this marketing strategy as '*commercial judo*'. It can also be dubbed as '*commercial diplomacy*'.

Many a times, prices were settled in Europe between the European steel mills and their suppliers before negotiations started in Japan. JSMs not only kept a constant watch on the developments but also engaged in proactive commercial diplomacy to ensure price settlement at the lowest possible level. This was the quality of work they put in at the pre-negotiation stage. If Europe was able to settle low price first, then the Japanese would tell their suppliers that the price had already been settled and they could offer the same to their suppliers. Since Japan bought a huge quantity in a consortium, the suppliers had little choice but to fall in line.

The next step was the negotiation of prices in Japan. It usually consisted of two rounds in Tokyo. In the first round, they would exchange views on the respective economies, supply and demand imbalance, production and consumption of steel in the world and Japan, health of the consuming industries, and some other broad parameters. This was the indicator of what the Japanese would finally do: push for lower prices or concede higher prices than the previous contract during the next round of negotiations. No price discussion took place at this stage.

Their aim in the second round was to get one of the suppliers to accept as low a price as possible. The carrot dangled before such a supplier who could help them in settling lower prices was a reward of more than a proportionate share of business volume. Usually one of the large Australian suppliers, like Hamersley or Mt. Newman, blinked first and took the lead in lowering prices as they had a large quantity to sell. Other suppliers were simply told that the price had already been set in Japan.

Of course, all suppliers were given an opportunity to become the price leader in case they were ready to drop the price first, thus giving an impression that their buying process was fair. They also brought in an *independent standard,* like the price settled in Europe, and offered the same to their suppliers to make their process look competitive, and, therefore, a global benchmark. Yet, within these constraints, a game of commercial judo was played by trying to influence the price in Europe where they were not themselves buying. This helped them to lower the prices in Japan. However, price could not always be settled first in Europe, and many times it had to be settled in Japan, which in turn became the standard for settling the price in Europe.

Smart Buying

The JSMs or their JTCs took an equity position in the iron ore mining companies in Australia, Brazil, and elsewhere and thus became privy to a lot of private information and intelligence as joint venture partners. This sometimes enabled them to influence the prices at the time of contract negotiations. They could also persuade their joint venture partners/suppliers to bring down the prices, when the other suppliers acted difficult.

Price Leader (Supplier)

All suppliers who did not accept lowering of the price had to be content with a proportionately smaller share of business. India, being a relatively smaller exporter compared to Australia, usually preferred to toe the line. The whole negotiation then revolved around volume of business and the trade-off India could achieve between the supply of high-grade Bailadila/ Bellary/Hospet ores, etc. on the one hand, and the low-grade ores from eastern India on the other.

Now of course, iron ore supply and demand situation has undergone a sea change as China has emerged the biggest importer resulting in skyrocketing of the prices. About 80% of the total exports from India are to China but the demand has started to come down with the onset of global recession. However, Japan was the undisputed king for the purchase of iron ore till the mid-1990s.

How India Buys

India needs to emulate such systems of buying and make it process-driven instead of transaction-driven. The Government Trading Companies (GTCs) are expected to buy after floating global tenders and simply pick up the lowest prequalified party for placing orders.

Commercial information is neither protected as a secret by the state nor the press. This has encouraged global suppliers and buyers to form cartels against India through a collective strength. It is unfortunate that India is at the receiving end of the cartels, both as a buyer and as a seller. Even the press is not helpful, as it takes pride in publishing secret information about the government intent.

Need to Fix Buying

The purchase divisions of GTCs do a global market research of the products they intend to buy around the time of floating tenders only, but there is need to increase the rigour of this process and converting the purchase into a year-long activity involving comprehensive research not only on prices and availability of the product but also the upstream and downstream products and a host of other factors that can affect prices and availability of the products.

The tender discipline and the attendant vigilance angle prevent the companies from negotiating contracts at lower prices outside the tenders to cool the market. This gives international cartels handle to increase prices. Indian GTCs need to play a bit of a commercial judo/diplomacy. The government systems should permit such doing, for which positive efforts must be made. There is a good chance of the government being thus persuaded in the current liberal regime.

MMTC had experimented with departing from the standard tender procedures, where in a year of tight supply in the mid-1990s, it simultaneously followed the route of buying in tenders, buying outside the tenders soon after the tender closed but at the same rate as settled in the last tender, and entering into long-term supply contracts but pricing the product at the time of the purchase. This strategy did not go unchallenged. MMTC faced an adjournment motion in the Parliament.

The minister concerned personally examined more than 100 files of the purchases and after satisfying himself defended MMTC strongly and praised the company's efforts to depart from the standard procedures for delivery of goods to the country. He requested the opposition and the mover of the resolution to withdraw the adjournment motion. It was withdrawn forthwith. No damage was done to anybody in the company for doing so.

However, the policy has been liberalised considerably since then, and it is time for the public sector to demand pursuing sound commercial buying practices followed by other countries like Japan and China, and stop being victims of the international cartels.

Limitations of the Tender System

The tender system has its merits and demerits. It is a good device to discover price. But the price, which is justified by the prevailing supply and demand gap, is vitiated by the presence of global cartels of buyers and sellers. To that extent, its usefulness as a price discovery mechanism of the justified and fair price is eroded. Many a times, it is exploited by the cartels, which go on increasing the price to India progressively with every tender. All that is achieved in such a system is to discover and recognise the ever-escalating prices and helplessness. This is specially the case in a year of tight supply.

But for this caveat, it imposes a good discipline for achieving fairness in awarding contracts, provided again that the prequalification and conditions of a tender are not manipulated in favour of certain suppliers and they guard against spurious quality, which does not always happen. All said and done, the tender system is good, provided there is a guard against its weaknesses.

Therefore, tendering should be used as just one of the many methods. Buying should be an year-long process. There should be a surprise element. The commercial information should be a closely guarded asset, and one should use other techniques of price discovery and settlement through commercial diplomacy.

The problem is that not only the government but the public sector companies are very comfortable with the tender system, though for different reasons. The government feels that it can avoid corruption. The public sector officers feel that if they buy through tenders, there will be no investigation against them, even if this results in purchases at exorbitant prices or sub-normal quality.

But while both the government and the public sector feel safe, it is not the best system for the country. The important thing is not merely to feel safe but to make wise purchase decisions. We need many weapons in our armoury and the tender could be only one such weapon.

However, it should be pointed out that though the process of buying iron ore by Japan was not by tender, yet it was very clean, honest, and transparent, and is recognised throughout the world as a model of integrity. Can India claim this reputation for the tender system? Just a food for thought.

Purchase processes, which do not follow the tender system, are not necessarily whimsical and corrupt, as is commonly believed in India. They follow a certain transparent process which has a much more rigorous discipline than the tender system. The world keeps on buying commodities or products at certain prices, which provide reliable benchmarks of prevailing prices at different points of time. The competitors might have bought in the recent past at a certain price; another buyer might have floated a tender in the recent past and established a price; there might have been a sudden spurt in the global demand accompanied with the shrinkage of global supply, pointing to the inevitability of steep increase in price. There are many such straws in the wind to indicate the right price, and there are universally accepted, transparent, and objective standards, like the price settlement of iron ore in Europe providing the basis for settling prices in Japan, etc. MMTC itself bought a large quantity of urea outside the tender, soon after they were closed, where the last tender itself provided the benchmark price.

It, however, does not mean that alternative systems are always free of corruption, but at the same time nobody can say for sure that the tender system is clean either. This depends on national character. However, the alternative process can be made very rigorous, disciplined, transparent and totally above the board. Japan placed orders with MMTC worth thousands of crore, but there has not even been one instance of the Japanese asking for favours, direct or indirect.

The Chinese System

China was the largest importer of fertilisers in the world, particularly urea. Sinochem bought on behalf of the Chinese Government. India was the second largest importer of urea in the world and MMTC was the only company importing it on behalf of the state till about 1995, when some other state undertakings were brought in to share the burden.

Despite the best efforts, Indians dealing with Sinochem failed to elicit any information or intent. Even during personal meetings with the chief during International Fertiliser Association Annual Conferences, the Chinese were cautious and kept their buying intentions close to their chest. Unlike the Indian media, the Chinese press too did not highlight their buying intentions.

Sometimes, Sinochem's London office would buy one or two ships from whosoever gave it at lower than the prevailing international prices, without inviting tenders. At other times, MMTC suspected that some Chinese traders based in Hong Kong were picking up vessels for Sinochem. They would make such random purchases without letting the world know it was scouting for buying a large quantity. This would sometimes prevent the global cartels from artificially raising the price of urea.

Having discovered and established low prices outside tenders, Sinochem would suddenly float a tender for large purchases and buy at the lower prices already established by it in random purchases. When it anticipated a global shortage, it would promptly sign long-term supply contracts at prices to be fixed in the future. Its capacity to combine the tender process with alternative price discovery mechanism of random purchases through Hong Kong or other foreign offices and long-term supply agreements, etc., was the secret of their success.

Glaring Contrast

MMTC once tried to cool down the price of urea by skipping purchase in a tender, as the purchase committee came to the conclusion that the international cartel members, acting in consultation and concert with each other, had artificially raised the prices to India. The Department of Fertilisers made a hue and cry that India needed a large quantity of urea and that the company had missed an opportunity of lifting some quantity in this tender.

The press learnt it, presumably from the government sources, and it made a noise about the so-called missed opportunity. It also learnt, presumably from the same source that now India had decided to import a much higher quantity of urea than originally planned. The publication of this confidential information only helped global cartels of suppliers to raise the prices still further. Actually, the missed opportunity was not the small quantity of urea, but the possibility of breaking the cartel of international suppliers and buying it at much lower prices.

A union minister convened a meeting that was attended by another union minister and his deputy minister, a few secretaries, other senior officers and the MMTC team, where it was decided that at least 3 million tons of urea must be procured in a short time, irrespective of the price. This was a far higher quantity than earlier advised through our ministry, which was represented in this meeting by the secretary only. In fact, they initially pitched their demand at 4.5 million tons, which they were told was unrealistic and not required in view of the stocks in the country.

Copies of the minutes were sent to the senior officers who attended the meeting and their departments containing the so-called secret information about the purchase intentions. This could have easily leaked by any source despite the fact that the minutes were dutifully marked 'top secret'.

In that year of tight supply of urea, China wanted to import about 4.5 million tons. MMTC had literally been fighting a battle for every ship in the high seas, and did land about 2.9 million tons in extremely trying circumstances. The competition between India and China, coupled with the revelation of India's intention to purchase 3 million tons, was the treat of life for the international cartels, which set the global urea prices on fire.

Had the government kept its buying intentions confidential, like China, and had the Chinese and Japanese methods of buying gently been followed, India would have been much better off.

Fixing India's Buying Process

The process of buying is defective and broken and there is a need for a serious debate about the right process of buying. It is unfortunate that despite being a large country, India is at the receiving end, and instead of calling the shots in the global market, it is paying exorbitant prices for major purchases.

The tender should not be the only method of price discovery, though this could be one method. We must retain an element of surprise and use some of the methods adopted by China and Japan. This could be coupled with long-term contracts, where proportionately higher quantity awards could be guaranteed to those suppliers which take a lead in reducing prices. Equity positions can be taken in the foreign supplier companies, and other methods adopted for controlling resources and commodities.

The most important thing is to procure the desired quantity at prices considered fair and justifiable in the context of the prevailing demand and supply gap.

However, whatever method of purchase is used, the buying intentions must be kept confidential and not simply marked 'top secret'. If the suppliers know the buying intentions in advance, as they do now, the game is given away to them before it begins.

India's purchase process and methods have assumed great significance as the global prices of commodities like food grains, fertilisers, metals, and crude oil, etc. shot up steeply during the first three quarters of 2008, pushing up the import bill. The prices have softened since October 2008. However, they can rise again.

Global competition for such resources is going to intensify. The trading and other commercial companies from the rich countries have already developed monopolies or oligopolies over seeds, fertilisers, food grains, land, and other commodities. Such global companies and their cartels are increasingly controlling the scarce resources of the world.

Private cartels, oligopolies, and monopolies only raise prices and exploit consumers at the first opportunity, which has serious implications for buyers of the developing world. It is a scary situation for India and the other developing world, where the majority of the poor live.

India needs to be proactive in fighting the battle for control of resources to ensure commodity supplies at reasonable and fair prices, and at better terms of trade. But not even a meaningful beginning has been made in this direction. India will not only have to buy wisely but will have to invest abroad aggressively in controlling the scarce resources of commodities, fertilisers, hydrocarbons like crude oil, oil seeds, minerals, metals, and other factors of production and services like land, knowledge, skilled manpower, technology, and scientific advances.

The need is to run fast; otherwise, the business entities in advanced nations might leave little to control.

9

Decision Making

WE ARE REQUIRED TO TAKE DECISIONS AT EVERY STEP. THEY can be routine, important or critical involving the life and death decisions of an enterprise. An organisation is merely the end-product of the sum total of the decisions taken and executed by it. Therefore, honing the decision-making skills is critical for the success of the managers and the organisations.

Framework of Decision Making

1. Before deciding, it is important to determine whether a decision is required at all. Why fix anything if is not broken and if fixed, will create more problems? For instance, a disgruntled inefficient manager demands a promotion and the boss concedes. The similarly placed and more capable managers ignored for promotion might legitimately feel de-motivated. The organisation might have been much better-off had the decision to promote

the disgruntled employee not been taken. One has to think in advance all the ramifications of a decision.

A management of a large Navratna PSE conceded to higher benefits and salary structure than permissible and signed the wage settlement agreement with the Unions. It thought it had thus averted a strike. However, the Board and the Government rejected the agreement and directed it to renegotiate. The top management was embarrassed as they lost face with the Unions, which found it embarrassing to explain it to their constituents. This resulted in a deadlock and the company was on the brink of a strike and a major loss of production. However, fortunately, a mutually agreed alternative solution was found to break the deadlock. The earlier decision to sign the wage settlement agreement should not have been taken in the first place, as even the Unions knew that their demands were against the policy applicable to the PSEs.

One came across many situations where it would have been better not to have taken decisions under pressure. Avoiding needless decisions saves a huge amount of executive time, turmoil and embarrassment.

2. There is a need to carefully understand the exact nature of the problem before rushing to give a decision. A decision should not be based on the symptoms of a problem but on the real problem behind the symptoms. Just as a medical practitioner cannot treat a patient effectively only by treating the fever, which may be an initial symptom of the real disease, a manager cannot take base a decision on the initial symptoms of a problem. He/she must analyse the real problem behind the symptoms. One has come across many cases where organisations keep providing symptomatic relief without ever solving the main problem. They rush from one crisis to another.

3. Before rushing to give a decision, one should analyse whether the situation occurs repeatedly. If so, it is best to lay

down a policy to tackle it. For instance, the inventory may pile up every year during the off season for a product like fertilisers, which has seasonal demand. Such a recurrent crisis has to be dealt with not by just solving it once but by laying down a policy to prevent its recurrence. This may require making a policy to give price discounts, longer and cheaper credit and increasing expenditure on customer contact during the off-season to boost the sales.

The story has already been narrated of a CEO of a company that manufactured urea, who prevented a recurrent crisis of inventory by laying down a policy—that at no point of time, it would have an inventory holding capacity in its factory of more than a few weeks production. The sales staff had to run to sell the material in the off-season. This proved a great decision to keep the inventory and the working capital low.

Similarly, in many companies, a sundry debtor's crisis recurs every year. This again calls for reducing the decision to a policy so that the future debtors are prevented from assuming crisis proportions; otherwise, we may be chasing high debtors all the time, resulting in very weak cash flow.

For formulating a policy for prevention of recurrence of this crisis, one has to review the company's credit policy, the processes of creating the customer, delivering the product/service, collecting the debtors from the customers, monitoring, responsibility and accountability norms, etc. A story has already been told about how MMTC tackled a crisis of dangerously high sundry debtors of about Rs. 1700 crore in this manner. The villain was a broken credit policy, lack of clear responsibility and accountability, and weak monitoring. A decision had to be taken to make a new policy and the rules to solve the problem and not just keep running to collect money from the customers.

A story has also been told earlier of an IT company, which ran into a sundry debtors crisis as customers refused to pay for 80% of the services sold. The villain was the broken work processes. Once a policy decision was taken to rectify these processes, things improved quickly. This analysis not only led to the prevention of recurrence of the sundry debtor crisis but it also transformed the critical processes of the company. This led to far-reaching decisions and changes in the company.

These companies succeeded because they not only treated the symptoms, but delved deep into the real problem behind the symptoms, which required decision. High sundry debtors were the symptom of a bigger problem of the broken work processes and defective policy and not the problem itself.

Reducing crisis and problems, which are likely to recur to a policy, diminishes the work considerably by making working very systematic. This enables even junior persons to take important decisions of repetitive nature, thus saving the valuable time of the senior management. Besides, as soon as the crisis recurs, people know beforehand what they need to do instead of running to the top management to make a decision. They don't have to invent the wheel repeatedly.

4. Every policy or rule needs to be reviewed, say in six months or a year, as the context in which it was formulated changes over time. Institutions which do not do this end up in becoming rule-bound and bureaucratic. The government is a typical example of this malaise. Even large private companies including some multinationals are not rid of this disease.

5. Over time, even the assumptions of the business of an enterprise or industry become outdated. They can impose serious constraints on its business as already mentioned in the story of PEC. A decision has to be taken to understand the new assumptions, challenge the old and outdated ones and replace

them with the new realistic assumptions. If this is not done, the very survival of a company or an industry can be at stake. Such decisions bring about structural changes of far-reaching significance.

6. The United States and India had a policy in place to tackle terrorist attacks. However, could they afford to apply the same policy after the attacks on the World Trade Towers in the USA and the attacks in Mumbai? Though they looked similar terrorist attacks, yet both the countries had to respond by making a different policy. Applying the old policy would not have sufficed as the nature of the attacks was qualitatively different and much more sinister. Therefore, one needs to analyse even similar-looking problems very carefully. The temptation may be to apply the old policy but this may not be the right prescription for such problems, which look similar but are different. In business too, we need to understand this fine distinction.

7. All decisions are not amenable to being reduced to a policy, as they are required to be taken on a case-to-case basis on their merits. They are one-off decisions presenting a peculiar problem or opportunity. Therefore, one has to take a specific decision in such cases. For instance, the decision of MMTC to set up the pig iron and steel plant was one such specific decision. This could not have been generalised or reduced to a policy or a rule. Such stand-alone decisions have to be taken on merits.

The important point is that one should have the awareness about the nature of the problem requiring a decision. It is clear by now that one needs to analyse the events carefully to determine the type of decision that would be appropriate for each event.

8. Effective decision making requires an organisation structure. For instance, in the case of MMTC, it consisted of the board of directors, and the board committees like the Investment Committee, Sales Purchase Committee, Directors' Committee, Departmental Promotion Committee, and Fortnightly Communication Meetings. It institutionalised decision making. We took most of our major decisions in these committees and meetings. This structure helped us to take momentous decisions involving multi-million dollar contracts expeditiously, even in the public sector setting, without inviting any investigation or criticism.

9. Effective management demands decisions on priorities: Whether to invest in this project or that or in this or that product line? Should we concentrate on three or four most important priorities or pursue many priorities? Which are the three or four most important priorities, considering the current context and the ground realities of the company? All such business questions demand decisions on priorities and trade-offs, which can either expand its frontiers or limit its progress. This choice can make a company a giant or a dwarf. Choice of priorities and trade-offs is one of the most critical areas of decision making. Before a decision can be taken, each problem must be analysed properly and discussed with the colleagues at an appropriate forum within the organisation structure of decision making.

10. One has to be decisive and not keep dithering, ever collecting data and analysing ad-infinitum. One has no time to boil the whole ocean. One must decide.

11. We should involve as many people as possible through building a consensus, so that they own these decisions and, therefore, implement them whole-heartedly. That is why PEC and MMTC held hundreds of communication sessions with their officers and staff. When a problem is discussed amongst

colleagues in an open and frank atmosphere where everybody's opinion is heard respectfully and all the pros and cons are brought at the table, duly verified in the market without any bias, the decisions thus arrived at are grounded in the reality of the market, the customer and the competence of the people who have to execute them.

12. Consensus has its limits. Sometimes a CEO or other senior officers have to be alone in taking a major decision, if they have strong reasons to differ from the rest of the team. One has to have the courage to take a different decision, if one has the conviction that there are solid reasons to do so. Sometimes, such decisions based on a strong conviction, can have a major impact on the fate of an organisation. In such cases, one should not hide behind a weak consensus, which could be purely due to *social pressure of the company*. But this is not a matter of authority of the decision maker; it is more a question of his/her assuming responsibility for the decision, which can sometimes be awesome, requiring a lot of courage. MMTC stuck to its decision to set up the pig iron/steel plant in spite of the opposition from many powerful quarters including the financial institutions, as it had the courage of its convictions.

13. All major decisions involve risk. That is why courage is very important in decision making. Effort has to be made to reduce the risk as far as possible. Some of the tools used by the companies to reduce risk include return on investment, payback period, net present value (NPV), internal rate of return (IRR), breakeven analysis and sensitivity analysis, etc. However, there is much more than financial analysis to asses which alternative to pursue. Broader strategic direction, mission and objectives have to be kept in mind. Any decision which goes against our mission and objectives is likely to take us away from our

mission. The harder we work at such a decision, the farther away we will be from the main mission.

Even compromises have to be considered towards the end, but they should move us closer to our mission and not away from it.

14. The team must develop alternative solutions or proposals. If there are no alternatives, there cannot be any sound decision. A company erred in two or three proposals of investment. Each investment proposal was offered as promising a very good rate of return and fared very well on the other tools mentioned previously. No alternatives were offered for any of these proposals. The management erred in accepting these proposals but they proved a failure as none of the promised financial parameters fructified. Fortunately, the investment was meagre as they were in the nature of pilot projects. It can lead to disaster if the investment is major. Therefore, decision makers must insist on their team to develop alternatives, weigh each of them on a comparative basis, validate them in the market and make sure that it is well within the competence of the people who have to execute it.

Besides, every compromise must ensure that the minimum expectation from a decision agreed by the group is met. One cannot compromise beyond this.

15. Once a decision is made, it should be defined and written very clearly to avoid any confusion. Define clearly who all must know this decision and make sure they all know the exact decision; who is responsible to take action on the decision; and the date by which the decision must be carried out and the resources and empowerment provided. If these are not done in time, there should be a feedback mechanism to know in advance to correct the situation. Many public sector and even private companies falter in this step.

A decision must be monitored in various stages of its execution and corrective steps taken in time. Many companies fail to monitor through the actual execution. Non-execution or half execution negates a decision, as it is as good as not having been made. In fact, half execution is worse as some resources would have been deployed to execute the decision, but wasted because of half execution.

Once the decision is actually executed in the market, a reaction and feedback of the market and the customer must be given to the authorities who took the decision, so that they can take remedial action if the decision itself required modification.

Most decisions are lost because either the resources and empowerment are not given in time, or the feedback of the customer or the market are not given to the decision makers, or because nobody bothers to monitor whether the decision was actually executed. Execution is the Achilles heel.

In the public sector environment, many decisions are lost because of preoccupation with new decisions. People forget the old decisions before they are executed. Most companies do not have a rigorous discipline in putting up and following up the unexecuted decisions over time. One has been a witness to many important decisions even of the boards of some Navratna companies getting lost under the thick blanket of new decisions, many of which themselves meet the same fate. New decisions drown the old decisions. Hence, the weak decision making and execution.

Decision is made only when it is executed properly at the right time. Policy makers, who think that their job is over after making a decision, are living in a delusion. The main job of a decision maker is to ensure that the decisions are well executed. This is the hardest part of decision making.

Finally, it is wise to keep this framework of decision making in mind till the process becomes a habit of the mind and one develops a gut feeling about what decisions should be taken.

Gut Decisions

A large number of executives take decisions from their gut. Something within them cautions them that the decision does not seem good even though the data and analysis strongly support it. Sometimes you may be convinced that a flash, which has dawned on you, is the right decision and it turns out to be right. Jack Welch, the famous CEO of the GE who was rated as the CEO of the twentieth century has even written a book under the title *Straight from the Gut*.

Our brain retains certain patterns of the past experience. When a similar situation arises in the future, it recognises a similar pattern that propels some people to instantly make a gut decision.

Our brain is also able to see and recognise similar patterns in different industries and cross-index and transfer them from one to the other. I was once a witness to the diamonds being auctioned in the State Emporium of the Kerala Government at Delhi, which normally stocks handicrafts made by the villagers. The stock of the diamonds was limited, but the way the ladies were pouncing to buy them, without even bothering about the quality and price amazed me. What struck me was that the public had assumed that since it was an outlet of the Government, it could neither cheat nor overcharge. Therefore, whoever could grab the precious stones would benefit. This was not the place where diamonds were normally bought and sold. Yet, these sold like hot cakes and within a few minutes the stock was exhausted.

Many years later, after joining MMTC, which sold gold to jewellers, I recollected the episode of the Kerala Emporium and we started holding domestic jewellery exhibitions in India where we sold the jewellery to the public after testing and hallmarking it for genuine purity. It was our gut feeling that since we were a 'Government Company', people would have faith in the purity of our jewellery and would prefer to buy it from us than from the private jewellers who did not then sell hallmarked jewellery.

Our exhibitions proved an instant success and the biggest halls of Delhi and Mumbai were overcrowded with customers. This launched us in the jewellery business within the country as distinct from the bullion business and exhibitions held abroad. We not only set up our own shops in the domestic tariff area but also at the international airports. Later on, this launched the company in silverware and in setting up retail showrooms for selling gold and studded jewellery in a joint venture with a private company. The central theme and unique selling proposition of these retail outlets was certified pure jewellery marketed by a Government Company. It was a concept borrowed from the Kerala Government's State Emporium. MMTC built a successful business on such cross-indexing of a commercial practice.

When the founder chairman of POSCO, General E Jung Park, who was trying to set up South Korea's first steel plant despaired, as no institution including the World Bank was ready to finance them as they did not have any expertise to make pig iron and steel, he retired to an island for a holiday in the United States for a few days. While he was having a stroll on the beach one day, he got a sudden flash that Japan owed blood money to South Korea on account of the atrocities perpetrated by Japan in the Second World War.

The Chairman instantly saw a ray of hope for financing his project through this route. He cut short his holiday and flew instead to Tokyo, where his contacts helped him to fix his meetings with the highest authorities of Japan. The Government of Japan agreed to finance the steel plant out of the blood money, provided the President of South Korea, Chung Hee Park agreed. The Chairman then flew back to Seoul and persuaded the President of South Korea to accept the blood money for financing POSCO for setting up the first steel plant in South Korea. This is how one of the biggest steel plants of the world was financed and set up.

Many years later, when the IDBI and other financial institutions refused to finance NINL, because MMTC lacked the expertise to manufacture steel, POSCO's example inspired us to keep persisting; and finally we did succeed in getting the necessary funding of about Rs. 1000 crore. This was a gut instinct — we believed that just as POSCO had ultimately managed the funding, we too will succeed one day.

Decision making is not an entirely scientific process. Feelings and emotions play an important part in decision making, consciously or subconsciously. It is best to balance the intellect with the emotions.

Gut decisions become more important and necessary, the more a person goes up in the decision making hierarchy. At this level, it is practically impossible to collect or analyse all the facts and data. The gut fills the void. One certainly cannot go entirely by gut because it can go wrong. I have taken a few successful decisions, which I can attribute to gut; but have taken a few wrong decisions too based on the same gut.

Practical Approach to Decision Making

A practical approach is to get as many relevant facts as possible and as soon and as economically as possible, and take decisions based on analysis if your gut also gives you the signal that the decision is right. Many a times, it pays to go module by module and go on improving with the realities of the market. We will never have the full and relevant facts and we do not have the luxury of boiling the ocean. This approach allows for making improvements as we gain understanding of the market.

Decision making involves dealing with uncertainty and risk. We cannot know in advance how our decision will pan out. That is why decision making requires courage more than ability. Yet, effort can be made for reducing the uncertainty and the risk by using some of the available tools.

Summing Up

Which approach to decision making should one follow? One should take the best of the various approaches which may be relevant in the peculiar context we are placed in, our ground realities, opportunities, peculiar constraints, and our overall vision, mission and objectives.

A good way for an organisation to improve performance in decision making is to reduce decision making to a process for which some rough and ready steps practised by us have been mentioned in this chapter. Each element of decision making can then be improved upon with practice, training in related decision-making tools, making improvements in the process itself, and learning from the past decisions in a systematic and sustained way. This can lead to better decision making not only by individuals but by the organisation as a whole. This can lead to continuous learning in decision making.

However, if after following this process, one feels that there is still something wrong with the decision one is going to take, it may be better to wait for some enlightenment. Gut has its place in decision making but is not reliable every time. Since all decisions primarily deal with the uncertainty and risk, every effort needs to be made to reduce the uncertainty and risk to an extent possible and that too as economically as possible. However, courage is very important in taking critical decisions.

Making an initial diagnosis and decision, and then progressively improving it in stages or modules as more facts come to light has a definite place in decision making. Management professionals have to go to the market to find out if the decisions taken are working on the ground or not. If the earlier decision is not working, it is their responsibility to change it and not defend it. False ego has no place in decision making.

It is prudent to start changing the decision making process of an organisation in small steps. It takes time to change the process and behaviour of so many individuals and groups. However, if we succeed in one department, operation or process, others in the organisation start recognising the benefits of the new process being tried. Then they automatically want to introduce the new process in their department too. Gradually, the ripple effects embrace the entire organisation or most of it.

Relevant useful readings on this subject include *The Practice of Management* by Peter F. Drucker (Harper Collins, 1954) and *Harvard Business Review on Decision Making* (Harvard Business School Publishing Corporation, 2001).

If I had the option to give only one suggestion, which will prove most useful to improve the careers of the young managers, it will be that they should read and practise the classics written by Peter F. Drucker. My favourites besides the above book are *The Effective Executive, Managing for Results, Innovation and Entrepreneurship, Managing for the Future, Management Challenges for the 21st Century, Management: Tasks, Responsibilities, Practices,* and *Managing in the Next Society. The Essential Drucker*, a selection from the works of Peter F. Drucker brought out by the Harvard Business School also deserves a place in the above list. You cannot find a deeper reservoir of management wisdom.

10

Dealing with Interference

MUCH HAS BEEN WRITTEN AND TALKED ABOUT POLITICAL and bureaucratic interference in the public sector, the latter being much less than what is made out to be. However, there is some political interference which could be routed through the bureaucrats, some of who tactfully handle it at their end, while others simply transfer these pressures. However, ego-driven interference by the bureaucrats is not uncommon.

Interference also takes place directly in the PSEs, where for some reasons, public sector officials tolerate or even encourage it. Some want out-of-turn or undeserved promotions, confirmation, extension, or reappointment. Some others form a nexus for ulterior motives.

There are times when a determined and adamant political executive may interfere even when some strong and honest PSE officials resist pressures. This is more prevalent in coalition politics. Even the prime minister can feel hedged and helpless in restraining a political executive who is a nominee of a powerful coalition partner having an agenda of its own. However, interference in the public sector can be tackled.

INTERFERENCE IN FINALISING COMMERCIAL CONTRACTS

I joined MMTC with the assurance of the then commerce minister, P Chidambaram, that there would be no interference in the discharge of the duties. Subsequent incumbents too honoured this commitment. However, one of them was more persistent but was not entertained. After completing my five-year term, I preferred not to extend my tenure.

I was confronted by a businessman at the behest of a politician who offered to secure special licences for PEC against the already rejected applications from the office of the CCI&E, now known as the Director General of Foreign Trade. He suggested that since such licences would command a premium in the market when they were sold, the company should contract with him to pay him 50% of the premium for the licences secured by him. Smelling a rat, his offer was rejected.

Later, it was learnt that the businessman had been involved in some investigations pertaining to import licences.

Insist on Speaking to the Minister Directly

While attending a conference in Tokyo, around 1990, an aide of the minister telephonically demanded my immediate return in order to settle a certain case expeditiously. When asked to be connected directly to the minister, he made a hasty retreat. He was just being holier than the Pope.

One of the best ways to prevent interference is to seek direct audience with the minister concerned. It is much easier to explain to the minister why a certain action cannot be taken.

Looking at the case on return to the capital, it was learnt that the government had stopped export benefits of a private party at the recommendation of PEC since this party had walked out of a contract for a major project in another country without completing obligations and litigation had been underway. It was likely that the minister wanted it to be settled out of court so that their export benefits like cash assistance could be released. Responding to a note from the concerned joint secretary, it was pointed out that no action could be taken since the case was sub judice. It was forwarded to the minister who simply signed it without seeking compliance.

Later, there was one more attempt to sort this matter out through another route but since the company remained firm, the matter was graciously dropped.

Most politicians would like to interfere only when they are sure their interference would be tolerated. They generally do not touch PSEs whose management would be politely firm and takes a principled stand.

Sometimes ministers and politicians cannot avoid referring people to the PSEs as they have compulsions. One has to be tactful and do the right thing because they are conscious of the fact that the PSEs have their own limitations. Yet, it is a job they are often forced to indulge into. The PSEs also do not have to take every request from a minister or the PMO very seriously. In fact, some of them would be happy if the request is rejected. This saves them embarrassment of saying 'no'. Justified requests have to be accepted anyway.

Some relatives and friends of VIP politicians become active as soon as he or she comes to power. It is doubtful if the concerned VIP is aware of the weight being thrown or the personal agendas being circulated to meet their own interests. All such requests, however, are treated purely on merit.

We explain to them why their request cannot be accepted. Most of them appreciate our position. Others are told the acceptance of the request would invite negative reaction that might prove embarrassing for their patrons. They usually do not persist after that.

One good rule to deal with such people is to explain how a decision not to accept requests serves their own self-interest. For instance, a politician has to be explained whether it is of political benefit to him or an embarrassment prevented. A politician understands this language at once.

In a way, there is political and bureaucratic interference only with the passive or active cooperation of the public sector executives. There could be some PSE officers who go out of their way to please their bosses or connive with the politicians and bureaucrats to share the spoils, while others try to please the boss to win an out-of-turn promotion or favour. Such officers demean themselves and damage the organisation they work for. The interests of the organisation should never be sacrificed.

I have had a pleasant and unobtrusive experience with most of the ministers who did not interfere and were gracious if their request could not be accommodated. Bureaucracy seldom interfered. In fact, it extended tremendous support. A small request off and on, a harmless recommendation that does not demoralise the rest of the organisation or a request made because of some pressure or compulsion but leaving it to the organisation to decide on merits the course of action cannot be called interference. Such requests can be accepted with grace.

The golden rule is that if a request from a friend, relative, or colleague is entertained there is no reason why the benefit should not be extended to the bureaucrats or politicians. There should be no exception to the rule. A slight deviation would tantamount to opening the door wide open to gross interference from all quarters. In such a case, the onus of interference is on the public sector.

The management of the PSEs should not arrogate to themselves alone the right to judge whether they are right or wrong. The minister or the bureaucrat also has the right to tell that they are wrong and ask them to set it right. In such cases, both the parties should try to convince each other. This cannot be termed interference. Sometimes the corporate managements might take wrong or questionable decisions. In that case, it is the duty of the minister not only to intervene but make sure the wrong is set aside.

Sometimes, there is a very thin dividing line between interference and perception of interference. Much depends on the intent of the parties and the personalities of the minister, the bureaucrat, and the PSE chief. A good guideline is to make sure that whatever compromise is arrived at after a discussion should be in the interest of the company and fair to employees.

However, it is the bounden duty of the PSE management to put its foot down, irrespective of who interferes, if it is convinced that it is mala fide and against the interests of the organisation. These are the decisions which the PSEs have to make themselves as they alone are ultimately answerable. The politicians and bureaucrats, who might have made these requests, are not likely to be there to hold the hands of the PSE officers when they are held accountable. This is because the ministers and bureaucrats are birds of passage and keep changing because of transfers or a change in the government.

The Ultimate Choice

When the interference becomes very blatant and repeated, the management should consider the possibility of quitting and seeking greener pastures which are available in plenty. This is a much better alternative than making compromises that result in investigations later and spoil their post retirement life.

But it is not necessary to quit. One just has to be ready to quit and develop this mindset.

It is practically impossible for any minister to sack a public sector employee unless and until he can prove gross negligence of duty or fraud against him/her. Therefore, those of the senior public sector executives who do not want to quit may just lie low, keep sending replies to various enquiries without getting *emotionally disturbed* and concentrate on producing results. Sooner or later the storm blows over and the coalition politics takes care of the situation as the minister himself may change. One can make a choice depending on one's temperament and situation.

One can tackle interference successfully provided one's own hands are clean and a uniform code of conduct is practised for the friends of one's own and those of the minister, bureaucrat, or the politician.

Antithesis of Leadership

It pays to stand up for your principles and values. Toadying to the powers that be is not only humiliating but can be dangerous at times and against the interests of the society and the nation. It certainly debilitates the organisation whose interests are supposed to be guarded. It is the antithesis of leadership.

EPILOGUE

THIS BOOK HIGHLIGHTS THE PROBLEMS FACED BY THE INDIAN public sector and offers solutions thereof. Two case studies of MMTC and PEC have been quoted, which exemplify my belief that the public sector companies can be turned around despite the proverbial hardships faced. It is possible to wade through the system with tact, diplomacy, courtesy, courage of convictions, and effective communication with the government, employees, and other stake-holders, provided one's own hands are clean and the management can provide a good and effective corporate governance.

The stories of NINL, MMTC, and PEC also show that it is not merely possible to turn around these companies but also lead them to ensure their future. If the government feels that a new project is in the interest of the company and the nation, it can even go out of its way to amend policies and procedures to enable the public sector to set up new companies, as evidenced by the NINL example. Even the guidelines of the BPE can be used flexibly so that a right decision is not sacrificed at the altar of an outdated one.

Many public sector stalwarts have succeeded despite the problems faced and many will do so in the future as well. However, a majority of the officers fear motivated investigations and many others cannot be expected to have either the qualities of a diplomat or the courage of a lion. There is a need for a framework which can be operated successfully by the ordinary and commonplace officers of any commercial enterprise. However, the present framework is seriously flawed in this respect.

Hence, it is imperative that the public sector itself should be reformed in a manner that the majority of the employees are able to perform effectively without fear. They should also have the autonomy to perform, the freedom and empowerment to invest and recruit the right quality of human resources, and also make other important decisions.

Moreover, such reforms should have a people-dimension, as people are the purpose of an organisation. A technical view of efficiency bereft of the interests of the people involved implied in the so-called Washington Consensus espoused by the IMF, is self-defeating in any country let alone a poor country like India. Developing countries that blindly followed recommendations of privatisation, etc. (made by the IMF), like Russia, Thailand, and Argentina, have already paid a heavy price and those that dared to differ like China, Taiwan, and South Korea have benefitted.

Some unconventional public sector reforms have been suggested around which it may be possible to hammer out a national consensus. These are aimed at the maximisation of the rate of return on a huge capital of more than Rs. 4 lakh crore already invested, granting autonomy, empowering and ensuring improvement of welfare. It is not necessary that the reforms should be looked at purely from the prism of bridging the fiscal deficit.

The suggested reforms include rectifying the seriously flawed process of recruitment for top jobs; bringing down the government stakes to below 50%; separating management control from the ownership; selling state equity to a wide array of retail investors, financial institutions and employees within a stretched time frame; ultimately transferring ownership to the employees, and setting up a SPV, in the meantime, to make all the above possible. An entrepreneurial solution to rehabilitate the surplus staff has also been offered. These solutions will be of great help and add a people-dimension to the reforms.

These solutions will also create the basic conditions of performance as they will remove the hurdles arising out of the public ownership. But it is not necessary that they will perform unless they can improve their corporate governance, administration, and management. Good corporate governance is a function of the quality of management.

I have suggested the formation of a new professional sector consisting of professionals from the public and private sector, scientists, researchers, and scholars to exploit the population dividend. This can be done through disinvestment. An institutional financial framework has also been outlined for the formation and growth of this sector.

The biggest beneficiary of the reforms would, perhaps, be the private sector because disinvestment in the manner and on the scale will deepen and broaden financial markets in a big way, thus giving a momentum to the development and spread of entrepreneurship on a scale never before witnessed in the country.

The kind of entrepreneurship unleashed in this manner will give the biggest boost to the development of the SMEs. Many job seekers will become job givers and create many more new opportunities. The proposal to create a new professional sector, consisting of surplus public sector staff, private professionals in all walks of life, scientists, researchers, copyright owners, patent holders, etc. will lead to a more inclusive society sharing the benefits of national development.

This shall help many to graduate to the level of middle class with major beneficial effects on the society. The middle class has always played a huge role in transforming the societies and governance across the globe. Creation of jobs in this manner will be beneficial in countries like India which will have the maximum number of young people, thanks to the demographics, and also be the best solution and guarantor of reduction and elimination of poverty, better health, and education.

I am sanguine that there are chances of a national consensus evolving around these proposals. The responses received in this connection, from various political parties, and individual politicians, are encouraging.

Disinvestment is the need of the hour and, hopefully, the constraints imposed by public ownership will go away some day to pave the way for the public sector to perform. Nothing has ever prevented the public sector to abide by the best corporate governance standards, adopting best global benchmarks of performance, managerial efficiency and effectiveness, as evidenced by the NALCO story.

Presently, a colossal amount of time of the public sector managers is spent on managing the government. Once the hurdles imposed by the state ownership go away, there will be a major shift in their attention from the government to the market, which is the source of profits. This will make the public sector much more profitable.

The public sector manager of the future will have to learn the same skills of management as the private sector manager and an entrepreneur has to imbibe. His/her primary responsibility will be to produce and deliver better and newer products and services at ever-decreasing costs and better quality, and upgrade the innovation skills and technology to launch new products and services, not only to meet the felt needs but also the unfelt needs of society. He/she will have to learn these skills, educate and re-educate all the time to keep abreast of the brave new world and exploit its opportunities.

They will have to learn to meet the demands of the young and attune management strategies accordingly, thanks to the new demographics of India that make it the youngest country. This is going to be one of the biggest challenges before the future managers. The companies which can make this an opportunity shall prosper. Others may not do so well.

These managers will also have to learn to unlearn the outdated working habits, attitudes, the mindsets, technologies, and knowledge. Learning and unlearning are important ingredients of right learning that have to be life-long.

The main responsibility of a commercial enterprise is to be commercial. It must conduct its affairs in such a manner that it produces enough surplus to meet all the costs of the current operations in the good and bad times including those of risk taking, depreciation, interest, taxes, and corporate social responsibility. Besides, profit should be adequate to provide scope for paying the dividends, making investments, and earning a reasonable rate of return on the capital employed. It should also be able to attract high-quality human capital and technology resources to ensure its future. The public sector enterprises too are commercial entities and they have to meet similar expectations of the society.

5 THINKINGS TO WIN

Pravin Rajpal

Challenge conventional wisdom; Fail and make mistakes; Don't play safe; Think out-of-the-box; Be a daydreamer; Be very different; Don't follow the beaten path; Go where no one has dared to go; Connect the unconnected; Think the unthinkable; Do the undoable; Follow the 'next' practice instead of best practice; Be creative; Blend arts and science; Make six new products instead of Six-Sigma; Strive for excellence; Follow your passions; Look for problems to innovate — Because these are some of the most important business insights from the rags-to-riches story of the world's richest billionaires and fortune 500 companies.

All these and many more important business insights are categorised in *Five Thinkings to Win. Five Thinkings* are to business, what the five senses are to a man.

ISBN: 978-81-87108-46-7

BLESSED TERESA OF KOLKATA

Sunita Kumar

Mother Teresa of Kolkata was a Roman Catholic nun who through sheer force of personality and belief had an enormous impact on the care of the poor, the sick and the dying. She recieved the Nobel Prize in 1979. Through her transcendental spirituality she amassed a workdwide constituency devoted to her aims: there are now some seven hundred and forty homes around the world dedicated to her causes.

This authorised pictorial history is a tribute to Mother Teresa's extraordinary achievements and had been compiled by her closest associate as a tribute for her first death anniversary. Using photographs from around the world, the majority of which have never been published before, it includes pictures of her as a young girl in Albania, addressing the US Senate, of her funeral, her simple tomb and the beatification. But the major part of the book follows the daily round of the sisters and focuses on the charismatic figure of Mother Teresa.

ISBN: 978-81-87107-45-3

HONEY I SHRUNK THE WORLD

Ignitee Digital Solutions

Looking for the best place to buy DVDs? Or are you researching for your thesis paper on semantic web applications? Whatever you're looking for, if it's in the digital space, you are most likely to find it in this essential global digital media handbook, *Honey I Shrunk the World.* Apart from offering a new insight into a hitherto unexplored domain, it shows us how small our world has truly become. The book holds a wealth of knowledge in the form of digital basics, internet and mobile statistics of countries around the world, list of must-see websites, trends and predictions in the digital space, news roundup, case studies of brands who walked the red carpet at various awards, detailed tables and glossary and much more. Go through this book at least once, and believe us when we say, you will e-volve! "Ignitee has done the impossible! They've condensed the World Wide Web and converted it into this delightful book" — Amitabh Kant, author of *Branding India;* CEO and MD, Delhi Mumbai Industrial Corridor Development Corporation.

ISBN: 978-93-80069-71-5

MAHAVASTU™

Vastushastri Khushdeep Bansal

Vastushastri Khushdeep Bansal has been actively practising Vastu for the past 18 years. Through his experience of over 10,000 case studies, involving some of India's top companies and families he has distilled the concept of MahaVastu™ — a purer, simpler yet more powerful system of Vastu. In this book he helps you learn how to apply MahaVastu™ to your life, to live with more happiness, love and prosperity.

How to get this fulfilment and why you are not able to make your dreams come true; these questions lead to a science which we term as MahaVastu™. MahaVastu™ is both an Art and a Science to achieve a balance between the activities you perform to achieve your goals and the energies of your Space which help you reach those goals. What Ayurveda is for body and Yoga is for mind likewise, MahaVastu™ is for Life.

ISBN: 978-93-80069-37-1